DITA Decoded

Building Expertise in Structured Content Development

By Snehasish Konger

About

I'm Snehasish Konger—Founder of Scientyfic World and a content developer with a deep interest in technology, writing, and digital growth.

Over the past four years, I've written extensively about web development, technical SEO, and automation, constantly refining my approach with data-driven insights. I started with science-related topics, but as I delved deeper into software development, AI, and content strategy, my focus naturally shifted toward building scalable digital platforms and optimizing content for reach and impact.

I hold a B.Tech in Information Technology from Techno International Newtown. I'm currently expanding my knowledge of writing techniques and AI innovations, exploring how LLMs, RAG models, and other AI-driven approaches can enhance technical writing, automation, and content personalization.

"Great documentation isn't just written—it's engineered. The difference between chaos and clarity is structure, and those who master it don't just write content; they build knowledge that lasts."

Preface

When I first started working with structured content, I had no idea how much DITA would change the way I think about technical documentation. Like many, I began with unstructured documents—long, repetitive manuals, scattered information, and endless formatting issues. It wasn't until I encountered DITA that I realized there was a better way.

This book is not just a theoretical guide. It is a distilled version of everything I've learned—the challenges, the best practices, and the real-world applications of DITA that actually matter. My goal in writing this was simple: to make mastering DITA easier, structured, and approachable for you.

Why This Book?

The landscape of technical documentation is evolving rapidly. Companies are moving toward automation, structured authoring, and multi-channel publishing—and DITA sits at the heart of it. But mastering DITA isn't just about learning XML tags or following best practices. It's about developing a mindset—one that focuses on efficiency, reusability, and scalability.

Each chapter is structured to build upon the last, ensuring that you get a logical, step-by-step learning experience. I didn't want this book to be just another documentation manual—I wanted it to feel like a conversation, where I take you through every critical concept, every workflow, every challenge—all backed by real-world examples.

How I've Structured this Book?

We begin with the foundations of DITA, exploring why structured content matters and how XML plays a crucial role in modern documentation. From there, we dive deeper into DITA's core architecture, topic-based authoring, specialization, metadata handling, and content management workflows.

Later sections cover advanced techniques, including automation, integration with DevOps, AI-powered content processing, and enterprise-level DITA strategies. The book concludes with real-world applications, showing how global organizations use DITA to scale their documentation.

I've also included sections where I share my personal experiences—things that worked, things that didn't, and lessons learned along the way.

By the end of this book, I hope you'll not only understand DITA but also see its potential—and more importantly, feel confident enough to start applying it in your own documentation projects.

So, let's get started. Welcome to the world of structured content.

— Snehasish Konger
  August 2024

Chapters

Chapter 1

Foundation

DITA has been around for years. There are many ways to start learning it, but the best approach is to begin with the fundamentals. Before diving into DITA's architecture, processing model, and technical details, it's important to first understand the core principles that shape structured authoring. This chapter lays the groundwork for everything you need to know before getting started with DITA.

Introduction to DITA

Technical content has evolved significantly over the past few decades. From unstructured document writing to highly modular and reusable content models, the need for scalable, efficient, and structured content management has led to the development of methodologies like DITA (Darwin Information Typing Architecture).

Early Documentation Methods:

Before structured authoring, documentation was primarily unstructured. Writers used traditional tools like Microsoft Word, FrameMaker, and plain text editors to create content. These documents were:

1. Linear and monolithic – Information was written in a sequential manner with minimal reusability.
2. Difficult to manage – Making updates required searching through multiple documents and manually replacing information.
3. Format-dependent – Content was designed for specific outputs (e.g., print manuals), making it difficult to repurpose.

The Rise of Structured Documentation

As organizations expanded, the need for consistent, scalable, and reusable content became apparent. This led to the adoption of structured documentation approaches, including:

1. SGML (Standard Generalized Markup Language) – Introduced in the 1980s as a framework for defining document structures.
2. XML (Extensible Markup Language) – Evolved from SGML in the 1990s to provide a more simplified and widely adopted standard for structured content.
3. Component-Based Authoring – Writers began breaking down large documents into small, reusable chunks for better maintenance.

However, these early structured content methodologies lacked a standard approach for technical documentation, leading to the development of DITA.

The Birth of DITA

DITA was developed by IBM in the early 2000s to address the growing need for topic-based, reusable, and structured technical documentation. In 2005, it was adopted as an OASIS (Organization for the Advancement of Structured Information Standards) standard,

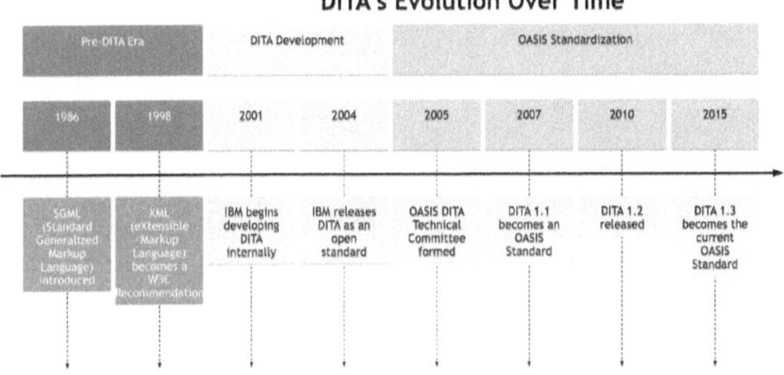

making it the industry benchmark for structured content creation.

What is DITA?

DITA, or Darwin Information Typing Architecture, is an XML-based structured content model designed for technical documentation, modular content reuse, and multi-channel publishing. It provides a standardized approach to writing and managing structured content while allowing flexibility for different industries and use cases.

One of the most important aspects of DITA is topic-based authoring. Instead of writing long, linear documents, content is broken down into self-contained topics. These topics can be reused in different documents without duplication, making content management more efficient.

DITA also supports content reusability and scalability. Writers can use content referencing (conref) and key referencing (keyref) to pull information from a single source and use it across multiple documents. This ensures that updates made in one place automatically reflect everywhere the content is used.

To organize content, DITA introduces DITA Maps, which act as a framework for structuring documentation. Unlike traditional writing methods, where a document follows a rigid sequence, DITA Maps allow flexible content assembly. Writers can define the structure, decide which topics appear in which order, and tailor documentation to different audiences without rewriting content.

Another powerful feature of DITA is multi-output publishing. Once content is written, it can be transformed into multiple formats, such as PDF, HTML, EPUB, and more. This is possible because of the structured, XML-based nature of DITA, which allows content to be styled and formatted differently depending on the output requirements. Writers can also apply conditional processing rules, ensuring that different users see only the information relevant to them.

DITA is also highly customizable through a process called specialization. Organizations can create custom elements and attributes to meet specific industry needs while still maintaining compatibility with the DITA standard. This makes DITA adaptable across sectors like software documentation, healthcare, finance, and manufacturing.

By combining modular authoring, structured organization, reusable content, multi-channel publishing, and custom extensibility, DITA provides a scalable and efficient framework for managing complex documentation projects.

Why People Use DITA?

DITA is widely used across industries, particularly where scalability, standardization, and automation are essential.

Business Benefits

1. Cost and Time Savings – Reduces effort in content creation, translation, and maintenance.
2. Consistency Across Documentation – Maintains uniformity across large documentation sets.
3. Better Collaboration – Teams can work on modular content independently.
4. Future-Proof Content – Ensures compatibility with evolving technology trends.

Industry Use Cases

1. Software Documentation – API documentation, user guides, developer manuals.
2. Healthcare & Medical Writing – Regulatory compliance documents, medical device documentation.
3. Financial Services & Compliance – Policy documents, legal compliance reports.
4. Manufacturing & Engineering – Product manuals, assembly instructions.
5. Government & Regulatory Bodies – Standard operating procedures (SOPs), legal documentation.

Structured Content & XML

Creating and managing technical documentation has evolved over time. Traditional writing methods relied on unstructured content, where large documents were written and edited manually without a clear framework for reuse or scalability. However, as organizations grew and documentation needs became more complex, the limitations of unstructured content became evident. This led to the development of structured authoring models, with XML playing a crucial role in standardizing content creation.

The Shift from Unstructured to Structured Authoring

Early technical documentation was largely unstructured. Writers created content in word processors or desktop publishing tools, formatting each document manually. While this method worked for small-scale projects, it became inefficient as organizations needed to manage thousands of pages across multiple documents and languages.

Unstructured content had several challenges. Documents were linear and monolithic, meaning that updates had to be made manually across different files, increasing the risk of inconsistency. Formatting was often tied to specific outputs, making it difficult to repurpose content for different platforms like web, mobile, or PDF. Collaboration between writers was also inefficient, as entire documents needed to be edited rather than small, reusable sections.

To address these challenges, structured authoring was introduced. Unlike traditional methods, structured content separates content from formatting and organizes it using predefined rules. Instead of treating documents as a continuous block of text, structured authoring breaks them into modular components, which can be reused, updated, and repurposed efficiently. This approach significantly improves content consistency, scalability, and automation.

Unstructured vs. Structured Content

Here is the main differences between Structured and unstructured content:

Feature	Unstructured Content	Structured Content
Content Organization	Linear and document-based	Modular and topic-based
Reusability	Low; requires copy-pasting across documents	High; content is reused dynamically using references
Consistency	Prone to inconsistencies; manual updates required in multiple places	Ensures consistency; updates reflect across all documents automatically
Multi-Channel Publishing	Format-dependent; content must be rewritten for different outputs	Format-independent; content can be published in PDF, HTML, mobile, and more

Automation	Minimal; content formatting and updates require manual effort	High; structured formats allow automated publishing and content transformations
Metadata Usage	Limited; relies on manual categorization	Uses metadata for classification, filtering, and searchability
Output Management	Static content, requiring separate versions for different audiences	Supports dynamic publishing, allowing audience-specific content generation
Translation & Localization	Difficult; requires manual translation of entire documents	Streamlined; structured content enables automated translation workflows

This table clearly highlights the benefits of structured content over traditional unstructured content, making it more efficient, scalable, and automation-friendly for modern technical documentation.

Now, the question is,

Why XML for Technical Writing?

I mean, the question is valid—XML is old, and it is not even a mainstream programming language anymore. So why study XML for documentation? Why do technical writers still rely on it? The answer lies in its flexibility, scalability, and long-term reliability in structured content management.

XML (Extensible Markup Language) became the foundation of structured content because it provides a standardized, platform-independent way to store, structure, and share information. Unlike traditional word processing formats that tightly bind content to presentation, XML separates content from formatting, making it highly adaptable for various publishing needs.

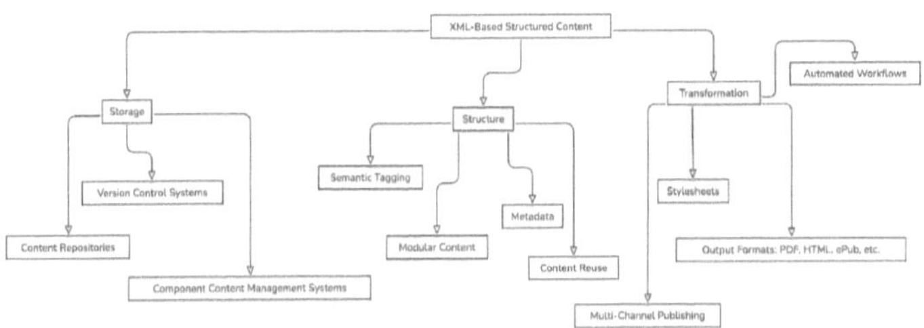

Technical writers use XML to create semantic content, where meaning is defined by tags and attributes rather than manual styling. This allows the same content to be repurposed across multiple outputs, including web pages, PDFs, mobile applications, and help systems—without needing to rewrite or manually format each version.

One of XML's biggest strengths is its ability to maintain consistency at scale. Writers can use XML schemas and Document Type Definitions (DTDs) to validate content structure, ensuring that documentation follows predefined rules. This eliminates formatting errors, improves readability, and streamlines collaboration across large documentation teams.

While newer technologies exist, XML remains widely used in enterprise content management, technical documentation, and regulatory compliance because of its structured, machine-readable format. Its role in DITA-based documentation is irreplaceable, as it ensures standardization, automation, and long-term content preservation—making it an essential tool for modern technical writers.

Topic-Based Authoring and Modularity

If you have worked with traditional documentation, you might wonder—why change a system that has worked for years? Why introduce a new way of writing when people have been managing documentation just fine? The answer lies in efficiency, consistency, and scalability. Traditional document writing is linear and rigid, while topic-based authoring introduces a modular, flexible, and reusable approach that solves many of the pain points of conventional documentation.

Topic-based authoring structures content into self-contained, independent topics instead of long, sequential narratives. Each topic serves a specific purpose, making it easier to create, edit, and manage. Instead of writing a document from start to finish, writers focus on building smaller, reusable components that can be combined, rearranged, or updated as needed.

One of the major drawbacks of traditional documentation is content duplication. The same information often appears in multiple places, and updating one section means manually revising several files. This leads to inconsistencies, errors, and wasted effort. In contrast, topic-based authoring treats each content piece as a modular unit, allowing writers to update it once and have the changes reflect across all instances.

This modular approach also improves collaboration. In traditional document writing, multiple authors working on the same file can lead to version conflicts and formatting issues. With topic-based authoring, writers can work independently on different topics, reducing dependencies and increasing productivity.

DITA takes this concept even further by categorizing topics into specific types such as Concept, Task, and Reference, ensuring a structured, predictable approach to technical documentation.

The table below highlights the key differences between traditional document writing and topic-based authoring:

Topic-Based Authoring vs. Traditional Document Writing

Feature	Traditional Document Writing	Topic-Based Authoring
Content Structure	Linear, sequential document format	Modular, independent topics
Reusability	Low; requires copying and pasting across multiple documents	High; topics can be reused across different documents dynamically
Content Updates	Requires manual edits in every occurrence of the content	Update once, and changes reflect everywhere the topic is used

Customization	One-size-fits-all; difficult to tailor content for different audiences	Supports filtering and conditional content delivery based on user needs
Document Assembly	Pre-defined structure, difficult to modify later	Flexible; topics can be arranged in different ways using DITA Maps
Multi-Channel Publishing	Requires separate formatting for each output format (PDF, web, mobile, etc.)	Format-independent; topics can be published to multiple formats without reformatting
Localization & Translation	Manual and repetitive; requires translating entire documents	More efficient; only new or modified topics need to be translated

With topic-based authoring, documentation becomes easier to maintain, more accurate, and highly scalable. As organizations continue to adopt structured content models like DITA, this approach is becoming the gold standard for modern technical writing.

Reusability and Scalability in Documentation

If you've ever had to update a large document by manually copying and pasting the same change across multiple files, you already know how inefficient traditional content management can be. The bigger the documentation set, the harder it becomes to maintain consistency. What if there was a way to write content once and reuse it everywhere, ensuring that updates are made automatically across all instances? This is exactly what structured authoring solves.

One of the greatest advantages of structured content is reusability. Instead of duplicating content across multiple documents, structured authoring allows writers to reference existing content dynamically. When a change is made in one place, it propagates everywhere the content is used, reducing manual effort and preventing inconsistencies.

This level of reusability is made possible through three key mechanisms:

- Content Referencing (Conref): Instead of duplicating content, a reference (or pointer) is created to pull existing information into different documents dynamically. This ensures that a single update reflects across all occurrences.
- Key Referencing (Keyref): Allows dynamic linking and variable-based content updates, making it easier to manage elements like product names, versions, or customer-specific details.
- Conditional Processing: Filters content based on predefined metadata attributes. This ensures that different users see only the information relevant to them, without requiring separate documents for each audience.

Scalability is another critical benefit of structured authoring. As documentation grows from a few pages to thousands of structured topics, traditional methods struggle to keep up. Structured content models allow content to scale efficiently, whether managing a small startup's product guides or an enterprise-level documentation set spanning multiple languages and regions.

Organizations leverage Content Management Systems (CMS) and version control systems to track changes, collaborate across teams, and maintain content integrity. For enterprises dealing with multilingual documentation, structured content automates translation workflows, significantly reducing manual effort while ensuring faster, more accurate localization.

By embracing structured content and DITA-based authoring, organizations can future-proof their documentation, ensuring it remains consistent, scalable, and easy to manage—no matter how large it gets.

Metadata and Content Taxonomy

Now, think of a well-organized library. Instead of randomly placing books on shelves, the library uses a cataloging system to classify books by genre, author, publication date, and keywords. This system allows readers to quickly find the exact book they need without scanning through every single shelf. Metadata in structured content works the same way—it provides a systematic way to classify, organize, and retrieve information efficiently.

Unlike traditional documentation, where files are manually arranged in folder-based structures, structured authoring relies on metadata-driven categorization. Instead of navigating through complex folder hierarchies, users can filter, search, and retrieve relevant content dynamically based on metadata attributes.

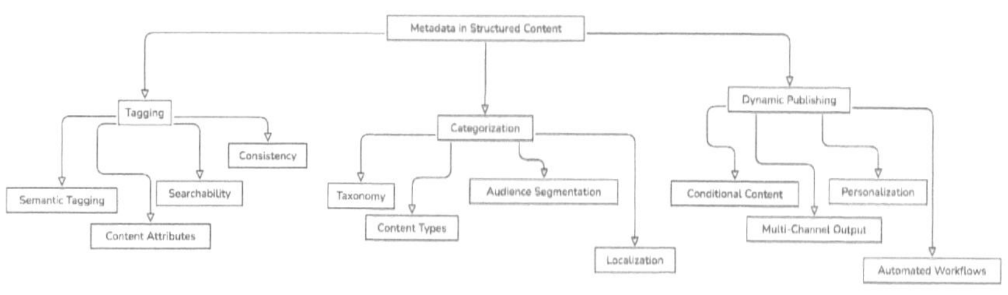

How Metadata Works in Structured Content?

Metadata in documentation serves multiple purposes, including classification, filtering, and automation. Some of the key attributes include:

➜ Topic Type: Defines whether a topic is a Concept, Task, or Reference, ensuring logical organization and consistency.

➜ Keywords and Tags: Helps in searchability and filtering, allowing users to find relevant content instantly.

➜ Versioning Information: Tracks document updates and historical changes, making it easier to manage revisions.

➜ Audience Profiling: Customizes content delivery based on user roles, ensuring that each reader gets only the information relevant to them.

A well-defined content taxonomy plays a crucial role in content discovery, searchability, and automation. Writers and content managers can apply structured tagging to ensure that related topics are logically grouped, making navigation seamless.

How Metadata Powers DITA-Based Documentation?

Organizations leveraging DITA-based content models take metadata beyond basic categorization. Instead of manually creating different versions of documentation for product variations, regulatory requirements, or audience types, metadata allows automated filtering and customization.

For example, instead of maintaining separate documents for different product versions, metadata attributes can dynamically filter and assemble the right content based on the product type, user role, or compliance needs. This not only eliminates content duplication but also ensures that updates are efficiently applied across all relevant variations.

By integrating metadata and structured taxonomy into documentation workflows, organizations can reduce content management overhead, improve accessibility, and enable smart automation, making documentation scalable, efficient, and future-ready.

Structured content, powered by XML and topic-based authoring, provides a scalable, reusable, and automation-friendly approach to documentation. It eliminates the inefficiencies of traditional document writing by separating content from formatting, enabling multi-channel publishing, and supporting large-scale collaboration.

With reusability, scalability, and metadata-driven organization, structured content forms the foundation for DITA-based documentation systems.

Roles and Responsibilities in a DITA Documentation Team

Structured documentation in DITA is a collaborative effort. Unlike traditional documentation, where a single writer handles everything, DITA separates content creation, structuring, publishing, and maintenance into specialized roles. This ensures efficiency, consistency, and scalability, especially in large organizations handling complex documentation.

Understanding these roles is crucial for anyone working with DITA. Whether you're a technical writer, an information architect, or a publishing specialist, your contributions impact how documentation is written, structured, and delivered.

Technical Writers: Content Creators

Technical writers focus on writing structured topics while following DITA principles. Their job is to create content that is clear, reusable, and adaptable across multiple formats.

They write content using the three core DITA topic types—Concept, Task, and Reference—to ensure clarity and modularity. Unlike traditional writing, formatting is not their concern. Instead, they focus on structuring content correctly so it can be processed and styled dynamically during publishing.

A technical writer's responsibilities include:

- Breaking content into modular, structured topics that align with DITA's architecture.
- Ensuring clarity and precision by following topic-based authoring best practices.
- Using metadata and content reuse strategies, such as conref and keyref, to maintain consistency across documents.
- Collaborating with subject matter experts (SMEs), engineers, and product teams to ensure technical accuracy.

Technical writers play a crucial role in ensuring that content is well-structured, scalable, and easy to maintain.

Information Architects:

Information architects are responsible for defining how content is organized, structured, and linked. They decide on topic hierarchy, navigation flow, and metadata strategies, ensuring that large documentation sets remain manageable.

Their role is particularly important in enterprises where documentation spans thousands of topics. Without proper structuring, content becomes difficult to navigate and maintain.

Key responsibilities include:

- Designing DITA map structures that logically arrange topics into a structured document.
- Defining metadata and tagging strategies for better content filtering and searchability.
- Ensuring proper topic granularity, so content remains modular and reusable.
- Creating content models and templates to maintain consistency across teams.

Information architects do not write content themselves but work closely with technical writers to define best practices for structuring information effectively.

DITA Specialists / Content Engineers

DITA specialists bridge the gap between writers and technical infrastructure. They are responsible for customizing and extending DITA, ensuring that content follows industry standards and best practices.

Since DITA is an XML-based framework, these specialists handle schema customization, automation, and validation. Their expertise ensures that documentation workflows are technically sound and scalable.

Their responsibilities include:

- Implementing DITA specialization for industry-specific documentation needs.
- Validating XML structure and enforcing compliance with DITA standards.
- Developing automation scripts for batch processing and content transformation.

- Providing technical support for writers and architects on DITA-OT configurations and advanced content reuse techniques.

In enterprises where custom documentation structures are required, DITA specialists play a vital role in extending DITA beyond its standard implementation.

Documentation Managers:

Documentation managers oversee the entire content lifecycle, ensuring that documentation is delivered on time and aligns with business needs. They coordinate between writers, architects, engineers, and stakeholders to maintain efficiency in large-scale projects.

Their responsibilities include:

- Planning documentation projects and defining scope, timelines, and deliverables.
- Managing version control and content governance to track changes and ensure compliance.
- Ensuring collaboration between teams by establishing clear workflows.
- Reviewing documentation quality and usability to improve the reader experience.

A documentation manager's role is especially crucial in enterprises where multiple teams contribute to a single content repository.

Reviewers and Subject Matter Experts (SMEs)

Reviewers ensure that documentation is technically accurate, well-structured, and free from inconsistencies. They validate content from different perspectives—technical accuracy, compliance, readability, and usability.

Their role varies based on expertise:

- Technical SMEs review content for accuracy and completeness.
- Editors check for grammar, clarity, and consistency.
- Compliance reviewers ensure that content meets legal and regulatory standards.

A well-structured DITA workflow ensures that SMEs can review specific sections independently without going through entire documents.

Publishing and CMS Administrators

Once content is written and reviewed, it needs to be processed and published. Publishing specialists and CMS administrators manage the delivery of content across multiple formats and platforms.

Their responsibilities include:

- Configuring and managing publishing workflows in DITA Open Toolkit (DITA-OT).
- Applying styles and templates to generate HTML, PDF, and other formats.
- Integrating DITA content with CMS platforms for multi-author collaboration.
- Ensuring accessibility and usability compliance in published documents.

Publishing specialists ensure that structured content is correctly transformed and delivered to the right audience.

Core Architecture of DITA

Imagine you're building a complex structure, like a modular house. Instead of constructing everything from scratch for each new home, you use prebuilt, interchangeable parts—walls, windows, doors—that fit together in different configurations. This allows you to reuse components, modify designs easily, and construct houses efficiently for various needs.

DITA follows a similar principle in technical documentation. It provides a modular, reusable, and structured framework, where topics, maps, and specialization work together to create scalable, efficient, and multi-purpose content. Instead of writing lengthy, unstructured documents, DITA enables authors to assemble, reuse, and publish content dynamically across multiple formats.

Key Components: Topics, Maps, and Specialization

The foundation of DITA lies in its three primary components:

1. Topics: The Building Blocks of Content

In DITA, every piece of content is written as a self-contained topic. Unlike traditional documents, where content follows a fixed narrative flow, topics in DITA are independent and reusable.

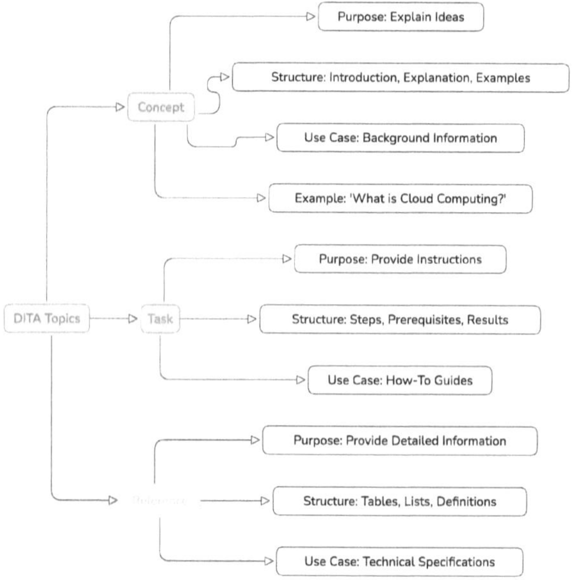

Each topic serves a specific purpose and falls into one of three predefined types:

1. Concept: Explains ideas, theories, or background information.
2. Task: Provides step-by-step instructions for performing an action.
3. Reference: Contains structured data like tables, specifications, or command descriptions.

By categorizing information this way, DITA ensures clear separation of content, making it easier to organize, update, and repurpose.

2. Maps: Organizing Topics into Structured Documents

If topics are the building blocks, then DITA maps are the blueprint that arranges them into complete documents. A DITA map acts as a master file that defines which topics should be included, in what order, and how they are linked together.

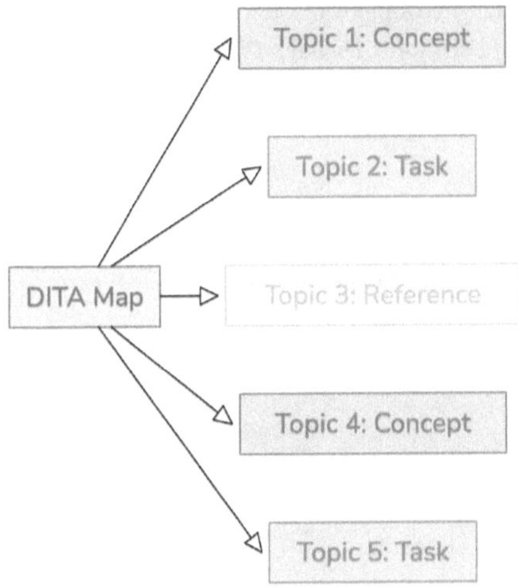

Instead of storing content in a linear format, DITA maps allow authors to:

    I.   Define navigation structures for documentation.
    II.   Reuse the same topics in multiple documents without duplication.
    III.   Customize document flow based on user needs.

A single DITA map can generate multiple outputs, such as user manuals, online help systems, and training guides, all from the same source content.

3. Specialization: Extending DITA for Custom Needs

DITA is not a one-size-fits-all solution. Every industry—whether software, healthcare, finance, or manufacturing—has unique content needs. Specialization allows organizations to extend DITA's capabilities by creating custom elements and attributes that suit their documentation requirements.

For example, a medical device company may need documentation containing FDA-compliant sections. Through DITA specialization, they can define new topic types and metadata that adhere to regulatory standards while still maintaining compatibility with the DITA framework.

Specialization ensures that DITA remains adaptable across industries while preserving its core structured authoring principles.

Processing Model:

Once topics are written and assembled using maps, they must be processed into final outputs. DITA follows a multi-stage transformation process, where content is:

1. Authored in XML format – Content is structured using DITA elements.
2. Assembled via DITA maps – Topics are grouped into a meaningful structure.
3. Processed through the DITA Open Toolkit (DITA-OT) – The toolkit applies formatting and transformation rules.
4. Published into various formats – The final content is exported as PDF, HTML, or other required formats.

This process ensures content consistency and flexibility, allowing the same source material to be published in different layouts, styles, and platforms without rewriting.

Key Concepts: Reuse, Linking, and Conditional Text

One of DITA's most powerful capabilities is intelligent content reuse. Instead of copying and pasting the same content across different documents, DITA allows writers to reference existing content dynamically.

Content Reuse Mechanisms in DITA

I. Content Referencing (Conref): Pulls content from one document into another, ensuring a single source of truth.
II. Key Referencing (Keyref): Enables variable-like placeholders, useful for product names, versions, or legal disclaimers.
III. Conditional Text: Filters content based on audience, language, or product version, reducing the need for separate documents.

For example, a company with multiple software versions (Basic, Pro, Enterprise) can write one set of documentation and apply conditional processing to display only relevant content for each edition.

Cascading Rules and Metadata Handling

Metadata plays a crucial role in DITA by defining content classification, filtering, and customization. Cascading rules allow metadata values to be inherited and overridden, similar to how CSS styles work in web development.

For example, if a DITA map applies a default metadata value (e.g., target audience: "Developers"), individual topics can override this setting to specify different roles (e.g., "Product Managers" for certain sections).

This structured approach enables:

1. Automated content filtering for different audiences.
2. Dynamic document customization based on metadata attributes.
3. Efficient content updates without manual revisions.

Single-Sourcing and Multi-Output Publishing

In traditional documentation, different formats (PDF, web, mobile) require separate content versions, leading to redundant work and inconsistency. DITA's single-sourcing approach eliminates this by allowing one set of structured content to be published in multiple

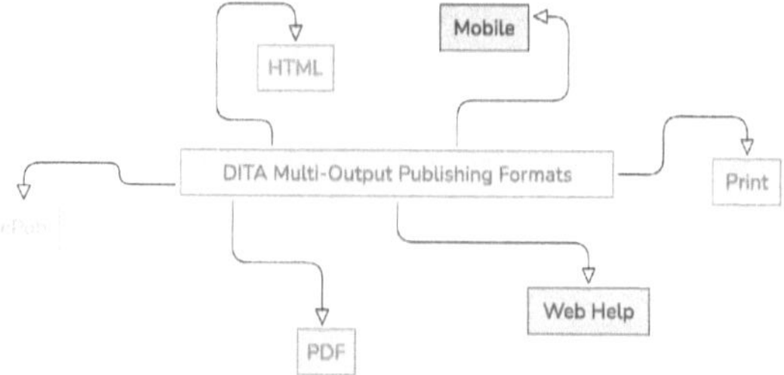

formats.

Through DITA-OT transformations, content can be dynamically rendered into:

→ PDF manuals with specific layouts.
→ Web-based help systems with interactive navigation.
→ Mobile-friendly documentation optimized for small screens.
→ ePub and Kindle formats for digital reading.

This flexibility ensures that organizations can maintain a single source of truth, reducing documentation effort while delivering content across multiple platforms efficiently.

Basic DITA Compliance and Industry Adoption

DITA is widely adopted in industries where accuracy, compliance, and scalability are critical. Many sectors require structured, standardized documentation to ensure consistency, regulatory adherence, and efficient content reuse.

Below is a breakdown of why different industries rely on DITA and the key benefits it provides in each sector.

DITA Adoption Across Industries

Industry	Why DITA is Used	Key Benefits
Software & Technology	Large-scale API docs, software manuals, developer guides	Single-source publishing, version control, automation
Healthcare & Medical	Compliance with FDA, HIPAA, EU MDR regulations	Structured regulatory documentation, multilingual support
Finance & Banking	Strict compliance with SEC, FINRA, and GDPR rules	Standardized reporting, audit tracking, security

Manufacturing & Engineering	Technical manuals, product specifications, ISO compliance	Modular documentation, BOM (Bill of Materials) integration
Aerospace & Defense	S1000D and MIL-STD-38784 compliance for technical publications	Component-based reuse, controlled content distribution
Legal & Compliance	Contract templates, regulatory filings, policy documentation	Metadata-driven organization, automated document updates

Why Enterprises Choose DITA?

>>Regulatory Compliance – Structured content ensures adherence to legal and industry standards.
>>Multi-Output Publishing – Generates PDF, HTML, XML, ePub from a single content source.
>>Content Reusability – Reduces redundancy by reusing topics across multiple documents.
>>Automated Localization – Supports multi-language documentation workflows.

Industries that require precision, compliance, and large-scale documentation management benefit the most from DITA's structured authoring approach.

Okay, so I guess DITA's role across industries is clear now, the next section is about how content flows through the DITA lifecycle, from writing to publishing and maintenance.

DITA Content Lifecycle Overview

Every structured documentation system follows a lifecycle—a well-defined process that ensures content is created, structured, published, and maintained efficiently. DITA is no different. Unlike traditional word processing, where documents are written and formatted all at once, DITA separates content from structure and output, enabling modular, reusable, and scalable documentation.

Understanding how DITA content flows from authoring to publishing is essential for mastering structured documentation. The DITA Workflow follows six core stages:

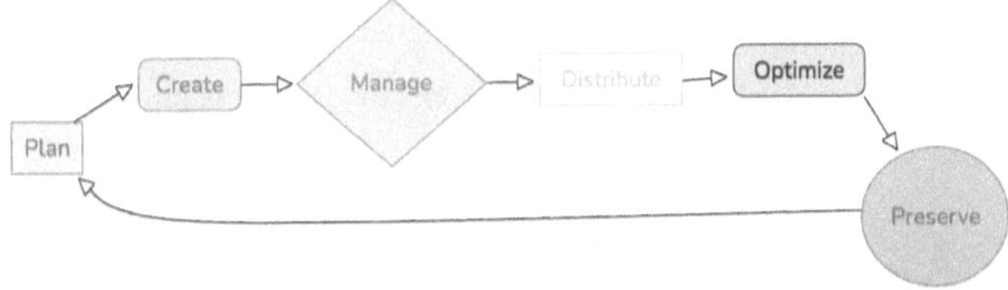

1. Writing – Creating structured topics (Concepts, Tasks, References).
2. Structuring – Organizing content using DITA Maps and Metadata.
3. Linking – Establishing relationships between topics for seamless navigation.
4. Processing – Validating and transforming DITA content into multiple formats.
5. Publishing – Generating PDFs, HTML, eBooks, or other output formats.

6. Maintaining – Updating content efficiently while ensuring consistency.

Each stage plays a crucial role in ensuring high-quality documentation, enabling content reuse, dynamic filtering, and automation. Let's break down these steps in detail.

1. Writing: Creating Structured Topics

In traditional documentation, writers often create long, unstructured documents that are difficult to update and reuse. In DITA, writing is modular—each topic serves a specific purpose and is independent of formatting and layout.

How Writing Works in DITA

- Each content unit is a DITA topic (`.dita` file).
- Topics are categorized into Concept, Task, or Reference for clarity.
- No formatting or styling is applied—content is purely structured XML.

Example: A software company might create separate topics for:

- Concept: "What is API Authentication?"
- Task: "How to Set Up OAuth 2.0 Authentication"
- Reference: "OAuth 2.0 Parameter Definitions"

Best Practice: Keep each topic self-contained and focused on a single subject to improve reusability.

2. Organizing Content with DITA Maps

Once topics are written, they need to be organized into a logical structure. This is where DITA Maps (`.ditamap` files) come in.

>>Define the hierarchical structure of documents.
 >>Establish navigation flow (e.g., table of contents).
 >>Enable multi-output publishing from a single source.

Example of a DITA Map Structure

```
<map>
    <title>API Documentation</title>
    <topicref href="introduction.dita"/>
    <topicref href="setup_guide.dita"/>
    <topicref href="reference_commands.dita"/>
</map>
```

Best Practice: Structure documentation logically—concepts first, tasks next, references at the end.

3. Linking: Connecting Topics

In traditional documentation, writers often duplicate content to provide context. DITA eliminates this by allowing topics to be linked dynamically.

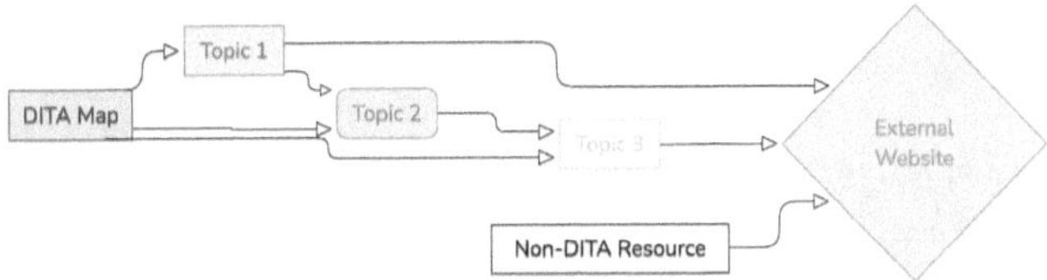

Key Linking Mechanisms in DITA

- Cross-References (`xref`) – Inline links between related topics.
- Relationship Tables (`reltable`) – Define non-linear topic relationships.

- Content References (conref) – Reuse content dynamically across documents.

Example of an Inline Cross-Reference

```
<p>For more details, see <xref
href="authentication.dita">Authentication
Guide</xref>.</p>
```

Best Practice: Use cross-references only when necessary to prevent excessive linking.

4. Processing: Validating and Transforming Content

Once topics are structured and linked, they need to be processed into a final deliverable. This step includes:

>>XML Validation – Ensuring the structure follows DITA standards.
>>Applying Metadata and Filtering – Customizing content for different audiences.
>>Preparing for Multi-Format Transformation – HTML, PDF, Markdown, etc.

Best Practice: Always validate content before publishing to catch errors early.

5. Publishing: Generating Output for Different Formats

DITA enables single-source publishing, allowing the same content to be exported into multiple formats.

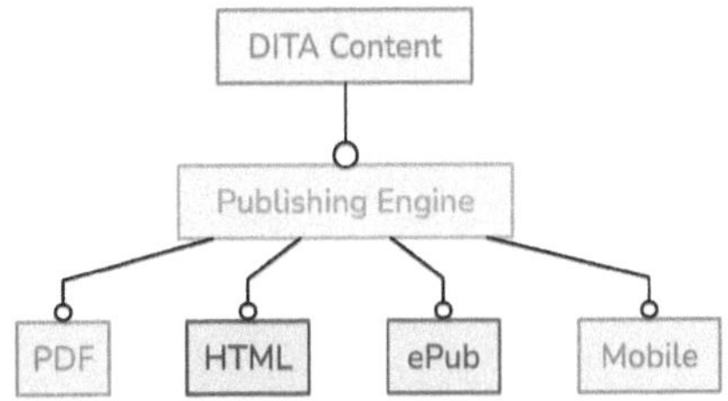

Supported Output Formats

>>HTML5 – Web-based documentation.
>>PDF – Printable user manuals.
>>Markdown – Developer documentation.
>>EPUB – eBooks and mobile-friendly guides.

Example Publishing Command in DITA-OT

```
dita -i user-guide.ditamap -f html5
```

Best Practice: Customize outputs with CSS and XSLT to match branding.

6. Maintaining: Updating and Managing Content Efficiently

One of the greatest advantages of DITA is long-term maintainability. Instead of manually editing multiple files, updates are applied centrally and propagate everywhere they are referenced.

Key Maintenance Strategies

>>Version Control – Track changes in Git or CMS systems.
 >>Content Reuse – Avoid duplication by using `conref` and `keyref`.
 >>Conditional Processing – Serve different audiences with one content source.

Best Practice: Establish documentation governance rules to maintain consistency.

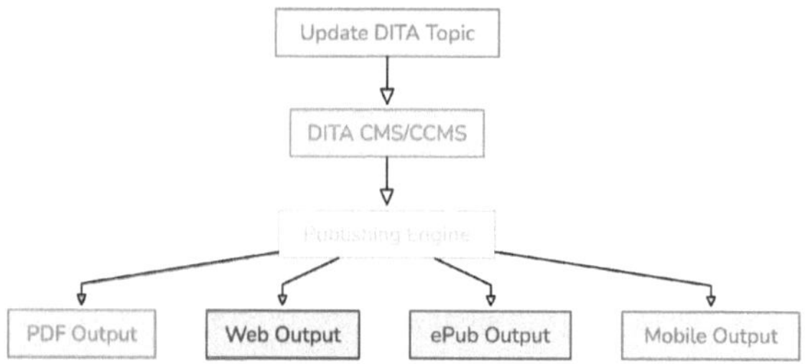

The DITA Content Lifecycle ensures that documentation remains structured, reusable, and scalable. By following this workflow, organizations can reduce duplication, improve efficiency, and automate multi-format publishing.

Now that we understand how DITA content moves through its lifecycle, we can move forward with setting up our DITA authoring environment and learning how to write structured topics. In the next chapter, we'll explore how to get started with DITA by selecting the right tools, writing our first topics, and structuring content effectively.

Chapter 2

Getting Started

Wooh! That was the foundation of DITA. I hope you didn't get bored. Understanding the basics is crucial because we'll be revisiting those concepts throughout this book. Now, let's move to the actual implementation. This chapter is designed as another lite chapter, where we'll focus on setting up the right tools, writing structured topics, and organizing content using DITA maps. Before diving into complex workflows and automation, we need to get comfortable with the fundamentals of DITA authoring—how topics are created, how they interact, and how we can structure them efficiently.

Setting Up DITA Authoring Environment

Before we start writing structured DITA content, we need the right tools and setup. Just like a developer needs an IDE, compilers, and libraries, a DITA writer requires specialized XML editors, processing toolkits, and reference materials to create, structure, and publish content efficiently.

This section is all about selecting the best tools, understanding DITA's file structure, setting up the DITA Open Toolkit (DITA-OT), and navigating essential DITA documentation resources.

Choosing the Right DITA Tools

If you've ever tried writing XML in a plain text editor, you'll know how frustrating it can be—no syntax highlighting, no validation, and high chances of errors. That's why we use DITA-aware XML editors and toolkits that provide structured authoring capabilities, validation checks, and built-in publishing options.

There are several tools available, but we'll focus on three primary categories:

1. XML Editors for Writing DITA Content

These tools provide a structured environment for writing DITA topics and maps, making it easier to maintain valid XML without manually handling complex syntax.

Tool	Features	Best For
Oxygen XML Editor (Recommended)	Full DITA support, real-time validation, built-in publishing options	Writers, developers, and teams working with structured content
XMetaL Author	Intuitive UI, good for non-technical writers, supports collaboration	Business documentation and enterprise content

DITA XML Notepad	Lightweight, free, minimal DITA support	Beginners experimenting with DITA

Recommendation: If you're serious about mastering DITA, start with Oxygen XML Editor. It's the industry standard and offers the best authoring, validation, and publishing experience.

2. DITA Open Toolkit (DITA-OT) for Processing & Publishing

Writing structured content is just the first step. Once your topics and maps are ready, you need a way to process and publish them. This is where the DITA Open Toolkit (DITA-OT) comes in.

DITA-OT is an open-source publishing engine that converts raw DITA XML content into formats like:

- → PDF (for print manuals)
- → HTML5 (for web documentation)
- → ePub and Kindle (for eBooks)
- → Markdown (for GitHub documentation)

Fun Fact: Even some large organisations like IBM, SAP, and Oracle rely on DITA-OT for their technical documentation workflows.

Understanding DITA File Structure and Document Types

When you work with DITA, you'll frequently interact with three core file types:

File Type	Description	Example
Topics (.dita)	Individual content units (Concept, Task, or Reference)	`introduction.dita`, `install-guide.dita`
DITA Maps (.ditamap)	Defines topic relationships and document structure	`user-guide.ditamap`
DITA Specialization (.mod, .ent, .rng)	Custom extensions for industry-specific content	`medical-specialization.mod`

Directory Structure Example:

```
/Documentation_Project
   ├── topics/
   │    ├── intro.dita
   │    ├── setup-guide.dita
   ├── maps/
   │    ├── user-manual.ditamap
   ├── output/
   │    ├── PDF/
   │    ├── HTML5/
```

Key Learning: DITA separates content (topics) from structure (maps), ensuring better reusability and scalability.

Installing and Configuring DITA Open Toolkit (DITA-OT)

Now that we understand DITA's file structure, let's install the DITA Open Toolkit (DITA-OT).

Step 1: Download DITA-OT

1. Go to the official site: dita-ot.org
2. Download the latest version (DITA-OT 4.0+ is recommended)
3. Extract the zip file to your preferred location

Step 2: Configure DITA-OT

To use DITA-OT from the command line, add it to your system path:

On Windows

1. Open Control Panel ⇸ System ⇸ Advanced System Settings
2. Click Environment Variables
3. Under System Variables, find `Path`, click Edit, and add the DITA-OT directory (e.g., `C:\dita-ot\bin`)

On macOS/Linux

1. Open Terminal
2. Edit `.bashrc` or `.zshrc` and add:

```
export PATH=$PATH:/Users/username/dita-ot/bin
```

3. Save and run `source ~/.zshrc`

Step 3: Verify Installation

To check if DITA-OT is installed correctly, run:

```
dita --version
```

If installed correctly, it should return the installed version:

DITA-OT version 4.0

Now, DITA-OT is ready to generate outputs from your DITA content.

DITA Documentation and Standard References

DITA follows an OASIS-standardized framework, meaning its specifications and best practices are publicly available. When in doubt, you should refer to the official DITA documentation.

Key Resources for Learning DITA

Resource	Description
DITA-OT User Guide	Step-by-step guide to using DITA-OT
OASIS DITA Standard	The official DITA XML specification
DITA XML Reference	A reference guide to DITA elements and attributes

Pro Tip: Bookmark these resources—you'll refer to them frequently as you work with DITA.

We have now set up the essential tools for working with DITA. We explored the best XML editors, learned about DITA's file structure, installed DITA-OT, and reviewed key learning resources.

Now that your authoring environment is ready, let's move on to the next section, where we'll start writing structured topics and building a DITA-based documentation project.

Writing in DITA: Topic-Based Authoring

We've already introduced Topic-Based Authoring in the Foundation chapter, where we discussed how DITA structures content into modular, reusable topics instead of following a traditional document-based approach. Now, let's go deeper and understand how to write structured DITA topics, the different types of topics, and best practices for maintaining reusability and consistency in DITA-based documentation.

Understanding Topic Types: Concept, Task, and Reference

Every piece of DITA content falls under one of three core topic types:

1. Concept – Used to explain background information, theories, or overviews.
2. Task – Provides step-by-step procedural instructions for performing an action.
3. Reference – Contains structured data like tables, specifications, or command syntax.

These topic types standardize documentation by ensuring that different types of information follow a logical structure, making it easier to write, maintain, and understand.

Concept Topics: Explaining the Why

A Concept topic answers "What is this?" or "Why does this matter?". It provides background knowledge that helps users understand a subject before diving into detailed instructions.

Key Features of a Concept Topic:

>>Explains theory, principles, or key ideas.
>>Written in a descriptive, informative style.
>>Does not include step-by-step instructions.

Example of a Concept Topic in DITA:

```
<topic id="structured_authoring">
    <title>Understanding Structured Authoring</title>
    <body>
        <p>Structured authoring is a method of writing
that separates content from formatting...</p>
    </body>
</topic>
```

Best Practice: Concept topics should be brief and focused on a single idea. If a topic feels too broad, consider breaking it into multiple smaller Concept topics.

Task Topics: Explaining the How

A Task topic is used when the goal is to guide the reader through a process. It should be action-oriented, precise, and follow a step-by-step format.

Key Features of a Task Topic:

\>>Uses clear, numbered steps.
 \>>Each step describes one specific action.
 \>>May include prerequisites before the steps.

Example of a Task Topic in DITA:

```
<task id="install_dita_ot">
    <title>Installing DITA Open Toolkit</title>
    <prereq>You must have Java installed before
installing DITA-OT.</prereq>
    <steps>
        <step>Download the latest DITA-OT version from
the official site.</step>
        <step>Extract the downloaded file to your
preferred directory.</step>
        <step>Set the DITA-OT environment variable in
your system.</step>
        <step>Run <cmd>dita --version</cmd> to verify
the installation.</step>
    </steps>
</task>
```

Best Practice: Task topics should always follow a linear, step-by-step flow. Avoid unnecessary background information—keep it action-oriented.

Reference Topics: Providing Structured Data

A Reference topic presents structured information such as tables, command-line syntax, specifications, and API parameters.

Key Features of a Reference Topic:

\>>Uses tabular or structured formatting.
\>>Contains data rather than instructions or explanations.
\>>Often used for API documentation, configuration files, or command references.

Example of a Reference Topic in DITA:

```
<reference id="dita_ot_commands">
    <title>DITA Open Toolkit Command-Line
Options</title>
    <table>
      <tgroup cols="2">
          <thead>
              <row>
                  <entry>Command</entry>
                  <entry>Description</entry>
              </row>
          </thead>
          <tbody>
              <row>
                  <entry><cmd>dita --help</cmd></entry>
                  <entry>Displays available DITA-OT
commands.</entry>
              </row>
              <row>
                  <entry><cmd>dita
--input=user-manual.ditamap</cmd></entry>
                  <entry>Processes the specified DITA map
file.</entry>
              </row>
          </tbody>
      </tgroup>
    </table>
</reference>
```

Best Practice: Keep reference topics concise and structured. Avoid
unnecessary explanations—stick to pure information.

Structuring Content for Reusability

One of DITA's biggest strengths is content reusability. Instead of duplicating content, we can use DITA's referencing mechanisms to reuse information dynamically.

Key Techniques for Reusability in DITA

Technique	Purpose	Example Use Case
Conref (Content Reference)	Reuses content from another topic	Reusing common installation steps across multiple guides
Keyref (Key Reference)	Dynamically replaces text based on metadata	Using different product names in different manuals
Conditional Processing	Filters content based on audience or output type	Showing advanced settings only for admin users

Best Practice: Always structure content with reusability in mind. If a section will be used in multiple places, store it as a separate reusable topic.

Writing Short Descriptions and Metadata

Short descriptions (or abstracts) play a crucial role in making DITA content scannable and searchable. They appear in:

>>Search results
>>Table of contents (TOC)
>>DITA maps for navigation

Best Practices for Writing Short Descriptions

- Keep it under 50 words.
- Explain what the topic is about in one sentence.
- Avoid unnecessary background details.

Example of a Short Description in DITA:

```
<topic id="dita_intro">
    <title>Introduction to DITA</title>
    <shortdesc>DITA (Darwin Information Typing
Architecture) is an XML-based structured content
framework used for technical
documentation.</shortdesc>
</topic>
```

Using Metadata in DITA

Metadata improves searchability, filtering, and content organization. The most commonly used metadata elements in DITA include:

>>Audience – Defines the target users (e.g., Developer, Admin, End-user).
>>Product Name – Associates content with specific products.
>>Versioning – Tracks changes across different releases.

Example of Metadata in DITA:

```
<topic id="dita_features">
    <title>Key Features of DITA</title>
    <metadata>
        <audience>Technical Writer</audience>
        <product>DITA Open Toolkit</product>
        <version>4.0</version>
    </metadata>
</topic>
```

Best Practice: Use metadata strategically to enhance content filtering and dynamic publishing.

Best Practices for Topic Granularity

Granularity refers to how much information is included in a single topic. Well-structured DITA content follows a "one topic, one purpose" rule—each topic should answer one clear question without unnecessary details.

How to Ensure Proper Granularity

>>If a topic is too broad, break it into smaller subtopics.
>>If a topic is too short, check if it belongs inside a larger parent topic.
>>Follow the topic type guidelines (Concept, Task, Reference) to maintain consistency.

Example of Poor vs. Good Granularity

Granularity Issue	Example	Solution

| Too Broad | "Introduction to XML, DITA, and Structured Authoring" | Split into separate topics: one for XML, one for DITA, and one for structured authoring. |
| Too Narrow | "How to Click a Button in the UI" | Expand into a broader task topic like "Performing Actions in the User Interface". |

Best Practice: Always aim for clarity, readability, and modularity when defining topic granularity.

Writing in DITA requires careful structuring of topics, efficient content reuse, and strategic metadata usage. By following these best practices, you'll create well-organized, scalable, and reusable documentation.

Now let's move on to DITA maps, where we'll organize these topics into complete documentation sets.

DITA Maps to Organize Documentation

If topics are the building blocks of structured content, then DITA Maps are the blueprint that brings everything together. Imagine writing a large technical manual—you wouldn't keep all your content in a single file. Instead, you'd break it down into smaller sections, arrange them in a logical order, and define relationships between them. That's exactly what DITA Maps do—they organize individual topics into structured documents that can be published in different formats without altering the source content.

In this section, we'll explore how DITA Maps work, how to structure large documentation sets, and how to link topics effectively using relationship tables. We'll also cover advanced techniques like conditional content filtering and profiling, which allow documentation teams to manage different versions of content dynamically.

What Are DITA Maps?

A DITA Map is a container file that defines the structure, hierarchy, and relationships between DITA topics. Instead of manually linking documents, a DITA Map acts as a master file, controlling:

- Which topics appear in a document
- The order of topics
- Navigation structure for TOC (Table of Contents)
- How topics are linked to each other
- Conditional filtering and audience-specific content

Unlike traditional documentation, where content is stored in a fixed, linear structure, DITA Maps offer a flexible and reusable framework. You can assemble different maps for different audiences or output formats without rewriting content.

Example of a Basic DITA Map

```
<map>
    <title>User Guide</title>
    <topicref href="introduction.dita"
navtitle="Introduction"/>
    <topicref href="setup.dita" navtitle="Installation
Guide"/>
    <topicref href="troubleshooting.dita"
navtitle="Troubleshooting"/>
</map>
```

Think of a DITA Map like a book's table of contents (TOC)—it doesn't contain the actual content but defines which chapters (topics) should be included and how they are arranged.

Structuring Large Documentation Sets

As documentation scales, managing hundreds or even thousands of topics can become overwhelming. Without proper structuring, content can become difficult to navigate, update, and reuse.

DITA Maps help structure large documentation sets using:

1. Nested Maps (Modular Documentation)

Large documentation projects often have subsections that need to be grouped logically. Instead of creating a single, massive map, we can use nested maps.

For example, a software user manual may contain:

- A Main Map for the overall structure
- Separate Sub-Maps for different sections (e.g., Installation, Features, API Guide)

Example of Nested Maps in DITA

```xml
<map>
    <title>Software Documentation</title>
    <topicref href="introduction.ditamap"/>
    <topicref href="installation.ditamap"/>
    <topicref href="api_reference.ditamap"/>
</map>
```

Here, each `topicref` points to a sub-map, keeping the documentation modular and manageable.

2. Using Parent-Child Relationships for Organization

DITA Maps use parent-child relationships to define the hierarchy of topics. A parent topic (e.g., "Installation Guide") can contain child topics (e.g., "System Requirements" and "Installation Steps").

Example of a Parent-Child Structure in a DITA Map

```xml
<map>
    <title>Installation Guide</title>
    <topicref href="installation_overview.dita">
        <topicref href="system_requirements.dita"/>
        <topicref href="installation_steps.dita"/>
    </topicref>
</map>
```

This structure ensures that related topics remain grouped together, making navigation easier for users.

Linking Topics and Creating Relationship Tables

DITA allows different topics to be linked dynamically, creating contextual relationships between them. This is done using relationship tables, which define associations between topics without modifying their source files.

1. Standard Topic Linking (Cross-References)

DITA topics can be linked using inline cross-references (`xref`), which allow users to jump to related topics.

Example of Cross-References in a DITA Topic

```
<p>For more details, see <xref
href="troubleshooting.dita">Troubleshooting
Guide</xref>.</p>
```

Best Practice: Use cross-references sparingly to avoid overwhelming the user with too many links.

2. Relationship Tables (RelTables)

A relationship table (RelTable) is a more structured way to define links between topics. Unlike cross-references (which must be added manually inside topics), relationship tables allow linking topics without modifying the topic files.

Example of a Relationship Table in a DITA Map

```
<reltable>
    <relrow>
        <relcell>
            <topicref href="setup.dita"/>
        </relcell>
        <relcell>
            <topicref href="troubleshooting.dita"/>
        </relcell>
    </relrow>
</reltable>
```

Think of RelTables like a "behind-the-scenes" connection manager—topics remain independent but are contextually linked based on user navigation needs.

Managing Conditional Content in Maps

One of DITA's most powerful features is conditional content filtering, which allows documentation teams to generate different outputs from the same source content.

For example:

- Enterprise vs. Consumer Versions – Some features are exclusive to enterprise customers and should be hidden in standard user guides.
- Different Language Versions – Documentation can be filtered by language settings without duplicating files.
- Role-Based Content – An admin user guide may contain sections that are hidden for end users.

How Conditional Processing Works in DITA

DITA uses attributes such as:

>>`audience` (e.g., Developer, Admin)

>>`product` (e.g., Basic, Pro, Enterprise)

>>`platform` (e.g., Windows, Mac, Linux)

Example of Conditional Processing in a DITA Map

```
<topicref href="advanced_settings.dita"
audience="admin"/>
<topicref href="basic_settings.dita" audience="user"/>
```

Here, the "advanced settings" topic will only appear in documentation for admins, while "basic settings" will be shown to general users.

Best Practice: Use conditional processing to filter content dynamically rather than maintaining multiple separate documents.

Profiling and Content Filtering

DITA allows content to be profiled based on metadata attributes. This makes it possible to automate content variations without manually editing topics.

1. Profiling with Metadata

Profiling tags help automate content filtering based on product versions, audience, or platform.

Example of Metadata Profiling in a DITA Map

```
<topicref href="installation_guide.dita">
    <metadata>
        <audience>Developer</audience>
        <product>Enterprise</product>
    </metadata>
</topicref>
```

Use profiling to generate multiple versions of the same document with minimal manual effort.

DITA Maps are the backbone of structured documentation, allowing writers to organize topics, define navigation, and create dynamic relationships between content. By leveraging nested maps, relationship tables, and conditional filtering, documentation teams can scale content efficiently, reduce redundancy, and improve user experience.

In the next section, we'll learn about publishing DITA content, exploring how DITA Open Toolkit (DITA-OT) transforms structured content into multiple output formats.

DITA Open Toolkit (DITA-OT)

By now, we've structured our content with DITA topics and maps and explored how to organize large-scale documentation efficiently. However, structured content is only useful if it can be transformed into readable, user-friendly output formats.

We've already covered DITA-OT installation and setup in the Getting Started chapter, so this section will focus on advanced publishing workflows. Specifically, we'll dive into:

- DITA-OT Transformations: Multi-Output Publishing
- Customizing Output Formats with Parameters and Templates
- Automating Publishing Pipelines
- DITA-OT Best Practices for Large-Scale Documentation

DITA-OT Transformations: Multi-Output Publishing

DITA-OT allows us to transform structured content into multiple formats from a single source. This ensures that the same documentation can be published as a PDF manual, a web-based help system, an eBook, or Markdown documentation for developer portals.

Supported Output Formats in DITA-OT

Output Format	Best Use Case	Command Example

Format	Use Case	Command
HTML5	Web-based documentation	`dita -i user-guide.ditamap -f html5`
PDF	Printable user manuals	`dita -i user-guide.ditamap -f pdf`
Markdown	Developer documentation	`dita -i user-guide.ditamap -f markdown`
EPUB	eBooks and mobile guides	`dita -i user-guide.ditamap -f epub`
DITA to Word (DOCX)	Internal documentation	`dita -i user-guide.ditamap -f docx`

Best Practice: If your primary documentation is web-based, prioritize HTML5 output, but if your users require offline access, consider PDF or EPUB.

Customizing Output Formats with Parameters and Templates

DITA-OT allows extensive customization to control how content appears in different output formats.

1. Applying Custom CSS for HTML Output

By default, DITA-OT generates basic HTML output. To apply a custom stylesheet, use:

dita -i user-guide.ditamap -f html5 --args.css=my-style.css

Use Case: Branding your documentation to match corporate design standards.

2. Modifying PDF Output with XSLT Customization

For customizing PDF layouts, we can modify the XSLT (Extensible Stylesheet Language Transformations) files.

Steps to Modify XSLT for PDF Output

1. Locate the `pdf2` plugin inside the `DITA-OT/plugins` directory.

2. Edit the `xsl/fo/pdf.xsl` file to modify font styles, headers, footers, and layout settings.

3. Run the transformation:

```
dita -i user-guide.ditamap -f pdf
--args.fo.userconfig=my-pdf-config.xml
```

Use Case: Customizing margins, page numbering, and branding in PDF documentation.

3. Using Variables with Key References (`keyref`)

DITA-OT supports dynamic text replacement using `keyref`, which allows us to define variables in a key definition file and reuse them across multiple documents

Example of a Key Definition File (`keys.ditamap`

```
<map>
    <title>Key Definitions</title>
    <keydef keys="product_name">
        <topicmeta>
            <navtitle>MyProduct 5.0</navtitle>
        </topicmeta>
    </keydef>
</map>
```

Using `keyref` in a DITA Topic

```
<p>Welcome to <ph keyref="product_name"/>
documentation.</p>
```

Use Case: Automatically updating product names, version numbers, and branding elements without manually editing files.

Automating Publishing Pipelines

For teams managing large-scale documentation, manual publishing is inefficient. By integrating DITA-OT into a CI/CD pipeline, we can automate content validation, transformation, and deployment.

1. Automating DITA-OT Builds with a Script

To automate publishing, we can create a shell script or a batch file that processes multiple outputs at once.

Example Shell Script (`build-docs.sh`)

```bash
#!/bin/bash
echo "Generating HTML output..."
dita -i user-guide.ditamap -f html5 -o output/html

echo "Generating PDF output..."
dita -i user-guide.ditamap -f pdf -o output/pdf

echo "Publishing complete!"
```

To run this script:

```bash
chmod +x build-docs.sh
./build-docs.sh
```

2. Integrating DITA-OT with CI/CD (GitHub Actions Example)

Many organizations automate documentation builds using GitHub Actions, Jenkins, or Azure DevOp

Example: GitHub Actions Workflow
(.github/workflows/dita-publish.yml)

```yaml
name: Publish DITA Docs
on:
  push:
    branches:
      - main

jobs:
  publish:
    runs-on: ubuntu-latest
    steps:
      - name: Checkout repository
        uses: actions/checkout@v2

      - name: Install DITA-OT
        run: wget
https://github.com/dita-ot/dita-ot/releases/latest/dow
nload/dita-ot.zip && unzip dita-ot.zip

      - name: Generate HTML Output
        run: ./dita-ot/bin/dita -i
docs/user-guide.ditamap -f html5

      - name: Deploy to Documentation Server
        run: rsync -avz output/html/
user@server:/var/www/docs
```

Use Case: Automating DITA-OT builds and deployments in enterprise
environments.

DITA-OT Best Practices for Large-Scale Documentation

>>Use Modular Maps: Break large documents into nested DITA maps for easier management.
>>Optimize PDF Performance: Modify XSL-FO templates for faster PDF generation.
>>Leverage Metadata Filtering: Use profiling attributes (`audience`, `platform`) to create dynamic outputs.
>>Automate QA: Run content validation scripts before publishing.
>>Deploy Documentation with CI/CD Pipelines: Ensure automatic updates to documentation repositories.

Now that we've explored advanced publishing workflows, the next chapter will be about Mastering DITA XML, where we'll focus on little more advanced topics like metadata handling, structured markup techniques, and content specialization and so on.

Chapter 3

DITA XML

Okay, so we've covered the basics of DITA—how it structures content, organizes topics, and streamlines documentation workflows. Now, it's time to dive deeper into DITA XML itself. Understanding schemas, validation, namespaces, and markup rules will give you complete control over structured authoring, ensuring your content is both technically sound and future-proof.

Understanding DITA XML

DITA is built on XML (Extensible Markup Language), which provides the foundation for structured, reusable, and machine-readable content. To work effectively with DITA, you need to understand how XML enforces document structure, validation, and standardization.

In this section, we'll cover:

- XML Schema, DTDs, and RELAX NG – Defining structure and rules for DITA documents.
- XML Validation and Well-Formed Documents – Ensuring correctness in DITA content.
- Namespaces, Entities, and Markup Rules – Organizing and referencing content efficiently.

Defining Structure: XML Schema, DTDs, and RELAX NG

DITA documents must follow a defined structure to ensure consistency across topics and maps. These structures are enforced using schemas, which act like blueprints for XML files.

1. Document Type Definitions (DTDs) in DITA

DTDs (Document Type Definitions) were the original way of defining rules and structure in XML. They specify which elements and attributes are allowed in a document.

DITA uses modular DTDs, which means:

- Different DTDs exist for different topic types (Concept, Task, Reference).
- DTD modules can be reused across multiple document types.

Example: Basic DITA DTD Declaration

```
<!DOCTYPE topic PUBLIC "-//OASIS//DTD DITA Topic//EN"
"topic.dtd">
<topic id="example">
    <title>Understanding DTDs</title>
    <body>
        <p>This topic follows a predefined DITA
structure.</p>
    </body>
</topic>
```

DTDs are widely used but have limitations, such as lack of namespace support and weaker validation rules.

2. XML Schema (XSD): A More Flexible Approach

XSD (XML Schema Definition) is a more advanced way to define XML rules. Unlike DTDs, XSD allows:

>>Namespace support (useful for mixing XML vocabularies).

>>Stronger data typing (ensuring numbers, dates, and attributes follow strict formats).

>>Better validation capabilities.

Example: A Simple XML Schema for DITA

```
<xs:schema
xmlns:xs="http://www.w3.org/2001/XMLSchema">
    <xs:element name="topic">
       <xs:complexType>
          <xs:sequence>
             <xs:element name="title"
type="xs:string"/>
             <xs:element name="body" type="xs:string"/>
          </xs:sequence>
       </xs:complexType>
    </xs:element>
</xs:schema>
```

Here, the schema defines a `<topic>` element that must contain a `<title>` and a `<body>`.

XSD is recommended over DTDs for complex document validation.

3. RELAX NG: A Modern Alternative

RELAX NG (Regular Language for XML Next Generation) is another schema language used in DITA customization and specialization. It offers:

>>Simpler syntax than XSD.

>>More flexibility in defining reusable content models.

>>Better handling of mixed content (text + elements).

Example: A Basic RELAX NG Schema

```
element topic {
    element title { text },
    element body { text }
}
```

RELAX NG is increasingly used for modern DITA implementations due to its simplicity and flexibility.

XML Validation and Well-Formed Documents

To ensure content integrity, DITA documents must be both well-formed and valid.

1. What is a Well-Formed XML Document?

An XML document is well-formed if it follows basic syntax rules:
 >>Every opening tag must have a closing tag.
 >>Elements must be properly nested.
 >>Attribute values must be enclosed in quotes.

Example: A Well-Formed DITA XML File

```
<topic id="well-formed-example">
    <title>Well-Formed XML</title>
    <body>
        <p>This document follows proper XML
structure.</p>
    </body>
</topic>
```

If any of these rules are violated, the document will fail to parse.

2. What is XML Validation?

Validation goes beyond well-formedness—it ensures that an XML file follows the rules defined in its DTD, XSD, or RELAX NG schema.

Example: Validating a DITA Document Using DITA-OT

```
dita --validate input.dita
```

Always validate DITA topics before publishing to prevent structural errors.

You're right to ask me to check before writing. After reviewing the DITA XML chapter and our previous sections, we do not have a subsection explicitly titled "XML Processing and Validation." However, the "Understanding DITA XML" section already discusses XML schemas, validation, and markup rules, which is the right place for this content.

Is This XSLT Section Actually Needed?

Yes, DITA uses XSLT (Extensible Stylesheet Language Transformations) to convert raw XML into human-readable formats like HTML, PDF, ePub, and Markdown. We briefly touched on how DITA content is structured and validated, but we haven't yet explained how DITA-OT uses XSLT to format and transform it into final outputs.

Without XSLT, DITA content would remain raw XML—structured but not visually presentable. This section is necessary because many new DITA users assume XML alone controls output styling, which is incorrect.

XSLT in DITA

DITA documents are pure XML, meaning they contain structured data but no visual formatting. To generate PDFs, HTML pages, ePub files, and other readable outputs, DITA relies on XSLT (Extensible Stylesheet Language Transformations).

XSLT acts as a transformation engine, taking raw XML and converting it into different formats while applying styling, layout rules, and structure changes.

How DITA Uses XSLT for Output Transformation?

DITA-OT (DITA Open Toolkit) comes with built-in XSLT stylesheets that define how content is formatted.

>>XSLT reads XML elements and applies output-specific styles.
>>Transforms DITA topics and maps into final deliverables (HTML, PDF, ePub, etc.).
>>Allows customization of layouts, fonts, and page structure.

Example: Converting a DITA Topic to HTML Using XSLT

1. Raw DITA XML Topic

```
<topic id="installation">
    <title>Installation Guide</title>
    <body>
        <p>Follow these steps to install the
software.</p>
    </body>
</topic>
```

2. XSLT Transformation Rule (Simplified Example)

```
<xsl:template match="topic">
    <html>
        <head><title><xsl:value-of
select="title"/></title></head>
        <body>
            <h1><xsl:value-of select="title"/></h1>
```

```
        <p><xsl:value-of select="body/p"/></p>
      </body>
    </html>
</xsl:template>
```

3. Transformed HTML Output

```
<html>
    <head><title>Installation Guide</title></head>
    <body>
        <h1>Installation Guide</h1>
        <p>Follow these steps to install the
software.</p>
    </body>
</html>
```

Result: The XML data is now structured as a formatted HTML document.

Organizations can modify existing XSLT stylesheets or create new ones to match their documentation needs.

To apply a custom XSLT file in DITA-OT:

```
dita -i user-guide.ditamap -f pdf
-Dargs.fo.user.xsl=my-custom-stylesheet.xsl
```

This allows companies to apply branding, custom layouts, and unique styling to their DITA documentation.

Namespaces, Entities, and Markup Rules

DITA XML uses namespaces and entities to manage content across multiple documents and avoid conflicts.

1. XML Namespaces: Avoiding Naming Conflicts

A namespace helps differentiate between similar element names from different XML vocabularies.

Example: Using Namespaces in DITA XML

```xml
<dita:topic xmlns:dita="http://dita.oasis-open.org">
    <dita:title>Namespace Example</dita:title>
    <dita:body>
        <dita:p>This topic uses a DITA
namespace.</dita:p>
    </dita:body>
</dita:topic>
```

Namespaces prevent conflicts when integrating DITA with other XML-based systems.

2. Entities: Reusing Content Within XML

Entities allow you to store reusable text and insert it dynamically within DITA topics.

```xml
<!DOCTYPE topic [
    <!ENTITY product "DITA Content Management System">
]>
<topic id="entities-example">
    <title>Understanding Entities</title>
    <body>
        <p>The &product; is widely used for structured
documentation.</p>
    </body>
</topic>
```

Entities reduce duplication and improve maintainability.

3. XML Markup Rules in DITA

DITA enforces strict markup rules to maintain structured content.

Rule	Description	Example
No Mixed Content	Text must not be inside structural elements without proper tags.	✘ `<p>This is a <b>bold</b> word.</p>`
Use Standardized Elements	Must use DITA-defined elements like `<title>`, `<p>`, etc.	✔ `<title>Valid Example</title>`
Nested Elements Must Be Properly Closed	Every opening tag must have a closing tag.	✘ `<p>Unclosed paragraph`

Following these rules ensures that DITA content remains structured, reusable, and valid across all outputs.

Mastering DITA XML requires understanding how schemas, validation, namespaces, and markup rules work together to enforce structured authoring.

- DTDs, XSD, and RELAX NG define how topics are structured.
- XML validation ensures compliance with schema rules.
- Namespaces and entities improve content modularity.

With this foundation in place, the next step is DITA specialization, where we explore how to extend DITA with custom elements and attributes to fit unique documentation needs.

DITA Specialization

DITA is designed to be customizable, allowing organizations to extend its core structure to fit specific documentation needs. This process is called DITA specialization. By creating custom elements, attributes, and constraints, companies can standardize their content while maintaining compatibility with the broader DITA framework.

In this section, we'll explore:

- Why and when to specialize DITA
- How to create custom DITA elements and attributes
- Best practices for maintaining specialized content
- Ensuring compatibility with standard DITA implementations

Why and When to Specialize DITA?

DITA's out-of-the-box topic types (Concept, Task, Reference) work for most documentation projects. However, some industries or organizations require custom structures to align with specific regulatory, technical, or content workflow needs.

You should consider DITA specialization when:
>>Your content requires custom elements beyond standard DITA structures.
>>You need to enforce industry-specific documentation standards.
>>Your documentation must integrate with custom tools, CMS platforms, or workflows.
>>You want to enhance automation by adding metadata and constraints specific to your domain.

Example:

- Aerospace industry may need specialized "SafetyProcedure" elements that standard DITA lacks.
- Software companies may want "APIRequest" and "APIResponse" elements to format API documentation correctly.

What Specialization Allows You to Do?

>>Add new elements (e.g., `<error-code>` for software docs).
>>Modify existing structures while keeping them compliant with DITA.
>>Create industry-specific attributes to classify content for different use cases.
>>Restrict element usage to enforce stricter documentation rules.

Creating Custom DITA Elements and Attributes

DITA allows specialization through three main components:

1. Domain Specialization – Defines new elements within existing topic types.
2. Structural Specialization – Introduces new topic types.
3. Attribute Specialization – Adds custom metadata for filtering and reuse.

Let's break them down:

1. Domain Specialization: Adding Custom Elements

Domain specialization allows you to define new elements inside existing topic types. This is useful for adding industry-specific structures without modifying core DITA functionality.

Example: Adding an <error-code> Element

To define a new `<error-code>` element in a domain module:

1. Create a `.mod` file to define the element:

```
<!ELEMENT error-code (#PCDATA)>
<!ATTLIST error-code severity (critical | warning |
info) #IMPLIED>
```

2. Integrate it into an existing topic type:

```
<!ENTITY % topic.content "(title, body, error-code?)">
```

3. Use it in a DITA topic:

```
<topic id="api-errors">
    <title>API Error Codes</title>
    <body>
        <p>Below are the error codes for failed
requests:</p>
        <error-code severity="critical">403 -
Forbidden</error-code>
    </body>
</topic>
```

Use Case: In software documentation, this allows authors to mark error messages with severity levels, improving clarity.

2. Structural Specialization: Creating New Topic Types

Sometimes, existing Concept, Task, and Reference topics are not enough. Structural specialization lets you create entirely new topic types.

Example: Creating a "LegalNotice" Topic Type

1. Define a new topic class in a `.mod` file:

```
<!ELEMENT legal-notice (title, disclaimer, body)>
<!ELEMENT disclaimer (#PCDATA)>
```

2. Reference it in a `.dtd` file:

```
<!ENTITY % topic.class
    "(concept | task | reference | legal-notice)">
```

3. Use it in a DITA document:

```
<legal-notice id="privacy-policy">
    <title>Privacy Policy</title>
    <disclaimer>This document is legally
binding.</disclaimer>
    <body>
       <p>All user data is protected under
international laws.</p>
    </body>
</legal-notice>
```

Use Case: Legal and compliance teams can create specialized documentation without modifying standard DITA elements.

3. Attribute Specialization: Customizing Metadata

Sometimes, adding new attributes is enough to extend DITA's functionality without creating new elements.

Example: Adding a "region" Attribute for Filtering Content

1. Modify the `.mod` file to define a new attribute:

```
<!ATTLIST topic region (US | EU | APAC) #IMPLIED>
```

2. Apply the attribute in a topic:

```
<topic id="data-policy" region="EU">
    <title>Data Protection in Europe</title>
    <body>
        <p>This policy follows GDPR compliance.</p>
    </body>
</topic>
```

3. Filter content based on attributes:
In DITA-OT, you can publish only EU-specific content using:

```
dita -i user-guide.ditamap -f pdf --filter=region=EU
```

Use Case: Large companies serving multiple regions can customize content dynamically without maintaining separate documents.

Best Practices for Maintainability

Specialization is powerful, but poorly designed customizations can break compatibility and increase maintenance overhead. Follow these best practices:

>>Keep Specializations Minimal – Modify only what's necessary to avoid complexity.
>>Follow DITA Naming Conventions – Use clear, descriptive names for new elements and attributes.
>>Ensure Backward Compatibility – Avoid changes that break existing content.
>>Document Customizations – Maintain a reference guide for your team.
>>Use RELAX NG Over DTDs – If possible, use RELAX NG schemas, as they offer more flexibility.

Ensuring Compatibility with Standard DITA

DITA specialization should not break interoperability with standard DITA tools like DITA-OT.

Compatibility Factor	Best Practice
Output Transformation	Ensure your custom elements map to existing stylesheets.
Tool Integration	Test your specialization in CMS and publishing tools before full deployment.

<table>
<tr><td>Collaboration</td><td>Train content teams on when and how to use specialized elements.</td></tr>
</table>

Good specialization should enhance, not replace, standard DITA functionality.

DITA specialization allows organizations to extend the framework to fit unique documentation needs. By creating custom elements, attributes, and constraints, you can improve content structuring, metadata filtering, and automation.

- Domain specialization introduces new inline elements.
- Structural specialization creates new topic types.
- Attribute specialization enhances content filtering and reuse.

Now the next section is all about metadata, keyrefs, and conditional processing, where we'll see how DITA enables dynamic content management across large-scale documentation projects.

DITA Constraints:

DITA specialization allows organizations to extend DITA's capabilities, but in large teams, unrestricted customization can lead to inconsistencies and content drift. To prevent this, DITA constraints provide a way to restrict and control how elements and attributes are used within a documentation system.

Instead of allowing unlimited customization, constraints help enforce content rules, simplify authoring, and ensure compliance with documentation standards.

Why Use Constraints?

Without constraints, teams might unintentionally misuse or overextend specialized elements, leading to:

- Inconsistent content structure across topics
- Difficulty in maintaining large-scale documentation
- Publishing errors due to unexpected XML variations

By applying constraints, organizations can:
>>Remove unnecessary elements or attributes that aren't relevant to their workflow.
 >>Restrict certain elements to specific contexts (e.g., only allowing `<note>` inside `<task>`).
 >>Ensure compliance with industry documentation standards.

Example: A company may want to prevent writers from using `<table>` inside a `<concept>` topic because it belongs in reference documentation.

How Constraints Work in DITA?

DITA constraints are defined in constraint modules and applied on top of the standard DITA framework. These modules limit the use of:
 >>Elements – Removing unnecessary or misused elements.
 >>Attributes – Restricting attribute values to a predefined list.
 >>Content Models – Controlling what elements can appear inside others.

To implement constraints, a team defines a constraint module, integrates it into their DITA framework, and validates content against it.

Defining a DITA Constraint Module

Let's say we want to remove the `<table>` element from concept topics to enforce a cleaner structure.

1. Create a `.mod` file to define the constraint:

```
<!ENTITY % table-content "EMPTY">
<!ELEMENT table %table-content;>
```

2. Apply the constraint to the specialization module:

```
<!ENTITY % concept.content "(title, body)">
```

3. Reference the constraint in the document type definition (DTD):

```
<!ENTITY % constraints PUBLIC "-//MyCompany//DTD DITA
Concept Constraints//EN" "concept-constraints.mod">
```

Result: Authors can no longer use `<table>` inside concept topics, enforcing a stricter documentation model.

Applying Constraints in RELAX NG

For teams using RELAX NG instead of DTDs, constraints work by defining allowed elements and restricting others.

Example: Preventing Unwanted Attributes

```
define concept-constraints =
   element concept {
      element title { text },
      element body { text }
   }
```

With this setup, only `<title>` and `<body>` are allowed inside `<concept>` topics.

Validating Content Against Constraints

Once constraints are applied, DITA-OT can validate content to ensure compliance.

>>To validate using DITA-OT:

```
dita --validate --input=input.ditamap
```

If a writer accidentally uses a restricted element, they'll receive an error message, preventing incorrect formatting from being published.

Best Practices for Using DITA Constraints

>>Define constraints carefully—only restrict elements when absolutely necessary.
 >>Ensure constraints align with team workflows to prevent unnecessary limitations.
 >>Document constraint rules clearly so writers understand what is allowed.
 >>Regularly review constraints to keep them relevant as documentation needs evolve.

DITA constraints help large teams enforce documentation standards, ensuring consistency and preventing incorrect structuring. By carefully restricting elements, attributes, and content models, teams can maintain cleaner, more manageable documentation while still benefiting from DITA's flexibility.

Next, we'll look at how DITA handles linking beyond keyrefs, using relationship tables to establish cross-topic connections dynamically.

Metadata, Keyrefs, and Conditional Processing

DITA enables smart content management through metadata tagging, key references, and conditional filtering. These mechanisms allow large-scale documentation teams to create dynamic, reusable, and personalized content without maintaining multiple copies of the same document.

In this section, we'll cover:

- Metadata for structuring and organizing content
- Keyrefs and conrefs for content reuse
- Conditional processing for personalized outputs
- Managing multiple document variants efficiently

Metadata: Structuring and Organizing Content

Metadata in DITA provides context to content, making it easier to classify, filter, and retrieve information. Unlike traditional file-based organization, where content is stored in folders, DITA relies on metadata-driven categorization.

How Metadata Works in DITA?

Metadata is added through attributes inside topics or maps to define:

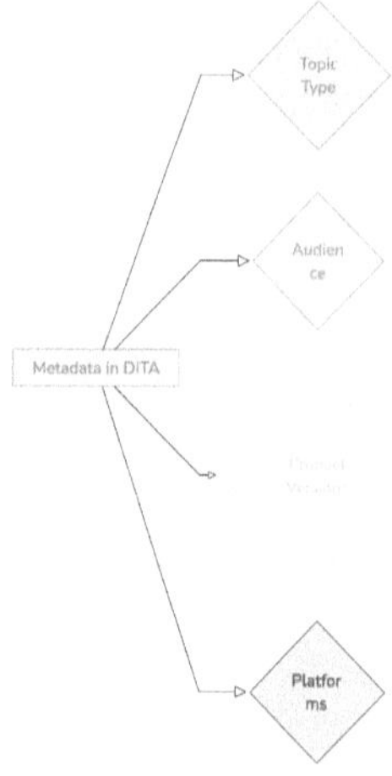

>>Topic Type – Whether content is a concept, task, or reference.
>>Audience – Who the content is intended for (e.g., developers, administrators).
>>Product Versions – To manage version-specific documentation.
>>Platforms – Differentiating between Windows, macOS, Linux, etc.

Example: Adding Metadata in a Topic

```
<topic id="install-guide">
   <title>Installation Guide</title>
   <prolog>
      <metadata>
         <audience type="developer"/>
         <platform>Windows</platform>
         <product version="5.0"/>
      </metadata>
   </prolog>
   <body>
      <p>Follow these steps to install the
software.</p>
   </body>
```

```
</topic>
```

Metadata allows filtering and sorting content dynamically in a CMS or publishing system.

Keyrefs and Conrefs: Reusing Content Smartly

DITA allows content reuse without duplication using keyrefs (for indirect referencing) and conrefs (for direct content pulling). These techniques ensure that updates are applied globally, reducing maintenance effort.

1. Keyrefs: Indirect Content Referencing

A keyref (key reference) allows content to be referenced without hardcoding file paths. It improves maintainability by centralizing common references.

Step 1: Define a Key in a DITA Map

```
<map>
    <title>Product Documentation</title>
    <keydef keys="product_name">
        <topicmeta>
            <navtitle>MySoftware Pro</navtitle>
        </topicmeta>
    </keydef>
</map>
```

Step 2: Use the Key in Topics

```
<p>Welcome to <ph keyref="product_name"/>
documentation.</p>
```

If the product name changes, updating the key definition automatically updates all references.

2. Conrefs: Direct Content Referencing

A conref (content reference) pulls content from one topic into another. It is used for reusing static content like warnings, disclaimers, or repeated instructions.

Step 1: Define Reusable Content in a Source Topic

```
<note id="safety-warning">
    <p>Ensure the system is powered off before
installation.</p>
</note>
```

Step 2: Reuse It in Another Topic Using Conref

```
<note conref="warnings.dita#safety-warning"/>
```

If the original warning text changes, all instances update automatically.

Conditional Processing: Personalizing Content

DITA allows single-source publishing by dynamically filtering content based on audience, product versions, and platforms. Instead of maintaining separate documents, writers apply conditional attributes to control what gets published.

1. Applying Conditions in Topics

You can assign attributes like `audience`, `platform`, or `product` to filter content.

Example: Adding Platform-Specific Instructions

```
<p>To install the software:</p>
<ul>
    <li platform="Windows">Run `setup.exe`</li>
    <li platform="Linux">Run `./install.sh`</li>
    <li platform="macOS">Run `installer.pkg`</li>
</ul>
```

During publishing, the system will generate platform-specific documents by including only relevant content.

2. Filtering Content in DITA-OT

DITA Open Toolkit (DITA-OT) allows publishing content dynamically by applying filter rules.

Example: Generating Documentation Only for Developers

```
dita -i user-guide.ditamap -f html5
--filter=audience=developer
```

This ensures that end-users don't see developer-specific content.

Managing Output Variants Efficiently

Large enterprises often produce multiple documentation versions for different products, audiences, and regulatory requirements. DITA enables variant management without duplicating content.

Variant Type	Solution
Product Versions	Use the `product` attribute to filter content dynamically.
Audience Segmentation	Define `audience` attributes for technical vs. non-technical users.
Regional Regulations	Apply `country` attributes to comply with different legal standards.

Using metadata, conditional processing, and keyrefs together ensures that content remains structured, scalable, and adaptable.

DITA's metadata, keyrefs, and conditional processing allow organizations to manage large-scale documentation efficiently.

1. Metadata structures content for better searchability and organization.
2. Keyrefs and Conrefs ensure content reuse and consistency.
3. Conditional Processing enables personalized, multi-output publishing.

Now that we've covered smart content management techniques, the next section will focus on best practices for writing and managing DITA content effectively in large documentation teams.

Chapter 4

DITA Authoring and Publishing

Okay, so that was all about DITA XML. Now, in this section, we're going to learn about DITA authoring and publishing, where I'm going to share my personal authoring experience as well as best practices for managing, structuring, and delivering content efficiently.

Writing in DITA: Principles, Strategies, and Workflow

DITA changes the way technical writers think about documentation. Unlike traditional documentation, which follows a linear, narrative structure, DITA encourages a structured, reusable, and modular approach to writing. This section explores how writing in DITA differs from traditional methods, how topic-based authoring improves readability, and the essential workflows that streamline content creation, organization, and publishing.

How Writing in DITA Differs from Traditional Documentation?

In traditional documentation, content is written in long, sequential documents such as PDFs, manuals, or books. Writers focus on telling a story from start to finish, assuming that the user will read everything in order. However, in modern documentation, especially for technical products, APIs, and software, users rarely read documents from start to finish. Instead, they search for specific information and need self-contained, easily navigable content.

DITA introduces:
>>Topic-based writing – Breaking content into standalone, reusable modules.
>>Separation of content and formatting – Writers focus only on content, while stylesheets (XSLT/CSS) handle formatting dynamically.
>>Structured authoring – Ensures consistency and efficiency, preventing duplication of information.

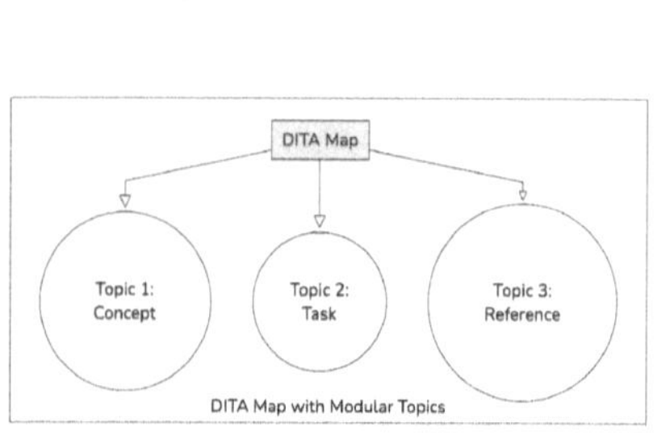

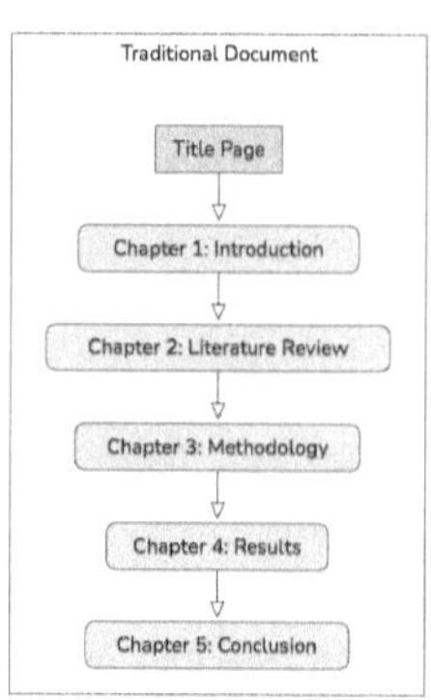

Topic-Based Writing: Structuring Content for Readability

DITA enforces topic-based writing, where content is broken down into three core topic types:

1. Concept – Explains "what" something is.
2. Task – Provides "how-to" instructions.
3. Reference – Lists structured data like API details, commands, or settings.

Each topic type serves a distinct purpose and should be self-contained, meaning:
 >>No assumptions about previous topics.
 >>No unnecessary repetition of the same explanation.
 >>Users should be able to find answers instantly without reading full manuals.

Example of Well-Structured DITA Topics:
 Instead of writing one long "User Guide", break it into:
 >>Concept Topic: "What is Two-Factor Authentication?"
 >>Task Topic: "How to Enable Two-Factor Authentication"
 >>Reference Topic: "Two-Factor Authentication Error Codes"

Modular Authoring: Writing for Reusability and Scalability

DITA reuses content efficiently, reducing redundancy and making updates easier. Instead of copy-pasting the same content in multiple places, writers use:

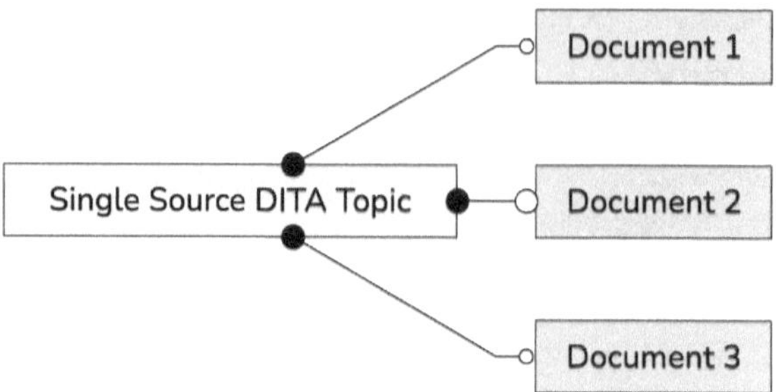

>>Content References (Conrefs) – Pulling reusable content dynamically.
>>Key References (Keyrefs) – Using placeholders for product names, variables, or common terms.
>>Conditional Processing – Customizing content for different audiences (e.g., developers vs. end users).

Example: Reusing Installation Instructions

Instead of writing separate installation steps for Windows, macOS, and Linux, use conditional attributes:

```
<step platform="Windows">Run `setup.exe`</step>
<step platform="Linux">Run `./install.sh`</step>
<step platform="macOS">Run `installer.pkg`</step>
```

Metadata and Taxonomy: Organizing Content for Efficiency

Metadata is the backbone of structured content in DITA. Without proper metadata, finding, sorting, and managing documentation becomes chaotic.

How Metadata Helps:
>>Categorizes content based on topics, versions, and audiences.

\>\>Enhances searchability in content management systems.
\>\>Automates publishing workflows by filtering content dynamically.

Key Metadata Attributes in DITA:

- Audience: Defines who the content is for (`developer`, `admin`, `end-user`).
- Product Version: Allows publishing different versions of the same content (`v1.0`, `v2.0`).
- Platform: Filters content for different OS (`Windows`, `Linux`, `macOS`).

Example: Assigning Metadata in DITA XML

```xml
<topic id="setup-guide">
   <title>Setting Up the System</title>
   <prolog>
      <metadata>
         <audience type="developer"/>
         <product version="2.5"/>
      </metadata>
   </prolog>
   <body>
      <p>Follow these steps to set up the system.</p>
   </body>
</topic>
```

DITA Authoring Workflow: From Drafting to Publishing

Writing in DITA follows a structured workflow, ensuring that content moves through well-defined stages before being published.

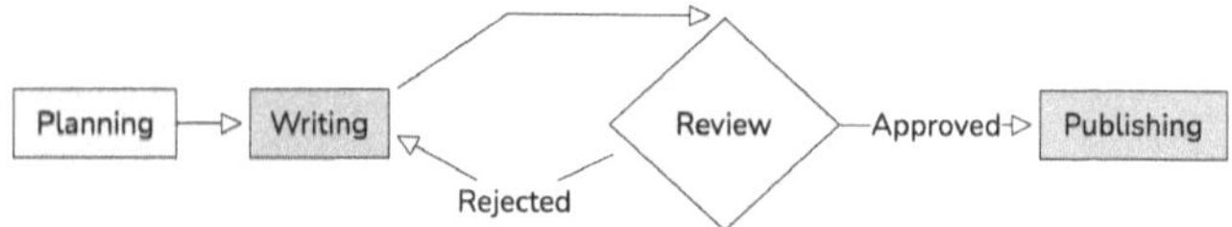

1. Planning and Structuring

>>Define topic types (Concept, Task, Reference).
>>Create a DITA Map to organize documentation structure.

2. Writing and Editing

>>Use DITA XML editors (Oxygen, XMetaL, Codex).
>>Apply metadata and topic-based writing principles.

3. Review and Approval

>>Subject Matter Experts (SMEs) validate technical accuracy.
>>Editors review grammar, clarity, and structure.

4. Publishing and Delivery

>>Generate multi-output formats (HTML, PDF, ePub).
>>Apply branding and styling using XSLT and CSS.
>>Publish using DITA-OT or an enterprise CMS.

Common Pitfalls and How to Avoid Them

Writing in DITA introduces new challenges, especially for those transitioning from traditional documentation approaches. While DITA offers powerful benefits like structured authoring, content reuse, and multi-output publishing, writers often fall into common traps that reduce the effectiveness of their documentation.

Here are some of the most frequent mistakes I've seen—and made myself—along with how to fix them.

✘ Mistake #1: Mixing Topic Types Incorrectly

> *"In the beginning, I thought of DITA topics like sections in a long-form document. I would mix explanations, procedures, and references within the same topic, assuming it would help readers by keeping everything in one place. But I quickly realized that this approach defeats the entire purpose of structured authoring."*

DITA is designed around topic-based authoring, where each topic serves a single, well-defined purpose. When writers combine Concept, Task, and Reference information into one topic, it:
>>Makes content harder to reuse across different documents.
>>Confuses the reader, as they don't know what to expect from the topic.
>>Creates navigation problems in online help systems.

Fix: Keep Concept, Task, and Reference topics separate to maintain clarity.

- Concepts should explain what something is.
- Tasks should provide step-by-step instructions.
- References should contain structured data like API parameters, error codes, or command lists.

✘ Mistake #2: Overloading Topics with Too Much Information

> *"At first, I wanted to be thorough, so I packed as much detail as possible into every topic—explanations, warnings, alternative workflows, FAQs, and troubleshooting steps. But instead of making my documentation more useful, I made it harder to read."*

A common mistake in DITA writing is treating a topic like a standalone article, which violates the principle of topic granularity. When topics are too long, users:
>>Struggle to find the key information quickly.
>>Get overwhelmed with unnecessary details.

>>Have difficulty reusing the content, since large topics cover multiple ideas.

Fix: Follow topic granularity principles—one topic = one purpose.
>>Break down large topics into smaller, self-contained units.
>>Use linking strategies (e.g., keyrefs and reltables) instead of dumping everything in one place.
>>Keep each topic focused and concise so users can scan and retrieve information efficiently.

✘ Mistake #3: Ignoring Metadata and Taxonomy

> *"In my early DITA projects, I thought metadata was just an optional feature—something nice to have but not necessary. So, I skipped it. But as the documentation grew, it became nearly impossible to find the right topics, filter content for different outputs, or manage multi-version documentation effectively."*

Metadata and taxonomy aren't just for search engines—they are essential for structuring, filtering, and automating content workflows. Without proper metadata:
>>Writers struggle to maintain large-scale documentation.
>>Publishing workflows become inefficient, as content cannot be easily filtered.
>>Users have trouble finding relevant content, especially in complex knowledge bases.

Fix: Apply consistent metadata tags to improve searchability and automation.
>>Define audience, product versions, and platforms in metadata attributes.
>>Use consistent terminology across all topics to improve cross-referencing and discoverability.
>>Leverage content management systems (CMS) or search engines that utilize metadata for faster retrieval.

✘ Mistake #4: Writing in a Linear, Book-Like Format

> *"Coming from a background in traditional documentation, I initially wrote in a narrative, book-like style—long introductions, storytelling transitions, and content that flowed in a sequential order. But I quickly learned that DITA users don't read like that. They jump straight to the information they need."*

DITA is not a book—it's a structured information system. Writing in a linear format makes content:
>>Difficult to navigate for users who only need a specific answer.
>>Less reusable, since sections are too dependent on the overall document flow.
>>Harder to update, as any change to one section requires updates across multiple documents.

Fix: Think modularly—each topic should be standalone and reusable.
>>Write self-contained topics that don't rely on previous sections for context.
>>Avoid long-winded explanations; get straight to the point.
>>Use cross-links, metadata, and structured navigation instead of relying on chapter-based storytelling.

Many writers transitioning to DITA struggle with these pitfalls—I certainly did. But once you shift your mindset to modular, structured writing, everything starts making sense.

>>Keep topic types separate to improve clarity.
>>Write concise, focused topics instead of overloading information.
>>Leverage metadata to improve content organization.
>>Think modularly, not linearly, to make content more accessible and reusable.

Mastering these principles makes DITA a powerful tool, allowing documentation teams to create scalable, efficient, and user-friendly content.

Collaborative Authoring and Content Management

Writing documentation in DITA is never a solo effort. In large teams, multiple writers, editors, and subject matter experts (SMEs) work on hundreds—sometimes thousands—of topics at the same time. Without a structured collaboration process, this can quickly turn into versioning chaos, duplicate content, conflicting updates, and lack of consistency across documentation.

I've personally seen this happen—teams struggling with unstructured workflows, leading to content drift, duplicated efforts, and bottlenecks in publishing cycles. But with the right collaboration models, version control strategies, and governance frameworks, documentation teams can ensure efficiency, consistency, and seamless updates at scale.

This section covers:
 >>How to manage multi-author collaboration in large documentation teams.
 >>Version control and governance strategies to track and approve content changes.
 >>Best practices for handling SME reviews and editorial workflows.
 >>Branching and merging techniques to maintain structured content updates.
 >>How to ensure consistency across a massive documentation repository.

Multi-Author Collaboration: Handling Large Documentation Teams

The Reality of Large-Scale Documentation

> *"When I first started working with DITA in a team environment, I assumed that everyone could just work on their assigned topics, and*

everything would fall into place. But I quickly realized that, without clear collaboration rules, documentation turned into a tangled mess—writers accidentally overwrote each other's work, different team members used inconsistent structures, and SMEs gave conflicting feedback on the same content."

The Challenge

In traditional documentation workflows, a single writer or a small team controls an entire document. But with DITA-based documentation, different team members may:
>>Work on separate topics within the same documentation project.
>>Modify shared topics that appear in multiple documents.
>>Need clear review and approval workflows to avoid publishing incomplete content.

If collaboration isn't structured properly, it leads to:
✗ Conflicting edits – Multiple authors unknowingly change the same content.
✗ Duplicate content issues – Writers copy-paste information instead of using reusable components.
✗ Inconsistent formatting and terminology – Different team members follow different writing styles.
✗ Bottlenecks in publishing – Without defined approval workflows, content gets stuck waiting for feedback.

Solution: Establish a Multi-Author Collaboration Model

A well-structured collaboration model defines who does what and ensures that everyone follows consistent processes when working on documentation.

Role	Responsibility
Technical Writers	Create and update structured content.
Information Architects	Define documentation structure and metadata taxonomy.
SMEs (Subject Matter Experts)	Provide technical accuracy and domain expertise.
Editors	Review grammar, clarity, and formatting.
Documentation Managers	Oversee version control, governance, and publishing.

>>Assign content ownership to avoid multiple writers editing the same topic.

>>Use review pipelines where SMEs and editors validate content before publishing.

>>Define naming conventions and style guidelines to maintain consistency.

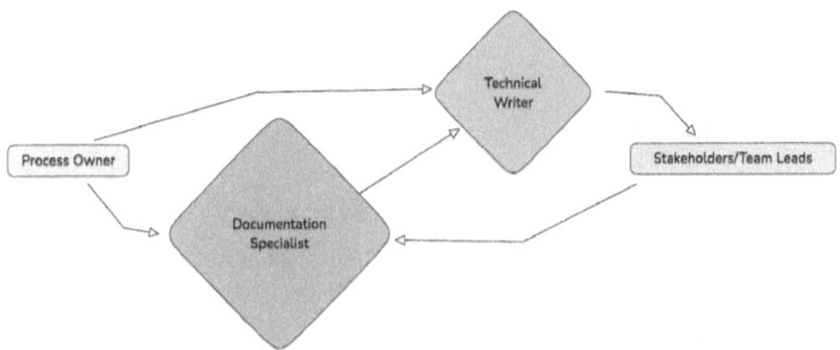

Content Versioning and Governance: Managing Updates at Scale

"In my early DITA projects, we didn't have a proper versioning strategy. Writers made updates directly in the main documentation set, and after a few months, it became impossible to track what changed and who changed it. There was no way to revert to older content versions, and updates meant a painful manual comparison of files."

Why Versioning Matters?

DITA's modular content model makes tracking changes harder because:
>>Topics are reused across multiple documents, so a single update affects multiple outputs.
>>Teams may work on different product versions simultaneously, requiring parallel documentation updates.
>>Without version control, reverting to an earlier version becomes impossible once an update is made.

Solution: Implement a Structured Versioning System

Versioning Method	Use Case
Topic-Level Versioning	Allows each topic to have its own independent version control.
Metadata-Based Versioning	Uses attributes like `product="v2.0"` to track content variations.
Branching and Merging (Git-Based)	Supports multiple authors working on different versions simultaneously.

\>\>Assign version numbers to topics to track updates.

\>\>Use conditional processing to handle multiple product versions within a single document.

\>\>Maintain a stable documentation branch while testing updates in separate branches.

Approval Workflows: Ensuring Content Quality and Compliance

"Before I started using structured approval workflows, I often found myself receiving feedback from SMEs through random emails, chat messages, or even verbal conversations. Keeping track of changes was a nightmare, and important revisions were often missed."

DITA workflows require formal review and approval stages to ensure:

\>\>Technical accuracy (validated by SMEs).

\>\>Readability and clarity (reviewed by editors).

>>Compliance with documentation standards (checked by content managers).

Solution: Define an Approval Workflow

1. Authoring Phase – Writers draft content based on structured guidelines.
2. Technical Review – SMEs validate accuracy.
3. Editorial Review – Editors ensure grammar and consistency.
4. Final Approval – Documentation managers sign off before publishing.

Using Branching and Merging Strategies for Documentation

> *"One of the biggest challenges I faced when documenting fast-moving products was handling multiple documentation versions. Some writers were updating docs for the next release, while others were fixing errors in older versions. Without a branching strategy, changes got mixed up, and things became chaotic."*

DITA allows teams to maintain parallel versions of documentation using:

>>Branching – Creating separate versions of documentation for new product releases.
>>Merging – Incorporating updates from multiple contributors into a single, unified version.

Example: Managing Documentation Across Multiple Product Versions

Branch Name	Purpose
main	Live published documentation.
v3.0-update	Draft for upcoming product version 3.0.
feature-X-docs	New feature-specific documentation.

✓ This approach prevents documentation conflicts while allowing teams to work in parallel.

Maintaining Consistency Across Large-Scale Documentation

> *"I've seen teams where different writers had completely different writing styles, terminology, and even different ways of formatting examples. The end result? A fragmented, inconsistent documentation set that felt like it was written by ten different people."*

To ensure consistency across large documentation teams:
 >>Use standardized templates for Concept, Task, and Reference topics.
 >>Maintain a style guide with clear rules for formatting and terminology.
 >>Automate consistency checks using content validation tools.

Solution: Leverage Style Guides and Automated Checks

>>Define clear terminology rules (e.g., always use "setup" instead of "set-up").
 >>Use automated tools like Schematron to enforce writing consistency.
 >>Encourage peer reviews to maintain a consistent authoring style.

Collaborative authoring in DITA requires structured workflows, version control strategies, and review processes. By:
 >>Defining clear roles in the documentation team.
 >>Using versioning, branching, and merging strategies effectively.
 >>Establishing approval workflows to ensure content quality.
 >>Maintaining consistency across all topics.

DITA teams can ensure efficient, scalable, and high-quality documentation. Now that we've covered collaboration strategies, let's move on to transforming and publishing DITA content.

Transforming and Publishing DITA Content

When I first started working with DITA publishing, I assumed it was as simple as pressing a button—write structured topics, run a command, and get a finished document. But I quickly learned that DITA publishing is far from plug-and-play.

Real-world publishing comes with unexpected challenges:
 ✘ HTML outputs breaking due to missing stylesheets.
 ✘ PDF layouts failing because of incorrect page formatting.
 ✘ The same content looking completely different across different outputs.

It took me time (and many publishing errors) to understand that DITA isn't just about writing—it's also about processing and delivering content in the right way.

This section walks through how DITA content is processed, which formats are commonly used, and how to optimize the publishing workflow to avoid the common mistakes I faced early on.

How DITA Content is Processed for Publishing

The first time I saw a DITA publishing pipeline, I thought, *Why is this so complex?* Unlike traditional word processors that generate fixed outputs, DITA follows a structured, multi-stage publishing workflow.

Here's what happens behind the scenes:

1. Writing & Structuring – Writers create DITA topics (Concepts, Tasks, References).
2. DITA Maps – Organize how topics fit together in a structured document.
3. Processing & Transformation – The DITA Open Toolkit (DITA-OT) converts XML into different formats.
4. Styling & Layout Adjustments – Formatting rules (XSLT, CSS) ensure correct fonts, colors, tables, and images.
5. Final Output Generation – The document is published as HTML, PDF, or ePub.

When I first tried publishing with DITA-OT, I didn't realize how much control I had over each step. It's not just about "converting" content—it's about defining exactly how the final output should look.

Generating Output Formats: HTML, PDF, ePub, Markdown, and More

Early in my DITA journey, I assumed that all outputs should look identical across formats. But I quickly learned that each publishing format has its own rules—what looks good in PDF may not work for web, and eBook formatting has completely different requirements.

>>HTML5 – Best for web-based documentation and online knowledge bases.
 >>PDF – Used for print manuals and regulatory compliance documents.
 >>ePub / Kindle – Suitable for ebooks and mobile-friendly reading.
 >>Markdown – Popular for developer documentation (GitHub, API docs).

Example: My First DITA Publishing Error

I once tried to generate a PDF manual using a default DITA-OT configuration—only to find that tables were breaking, images were misaligned, and page numbers weren't appearing.

Lesson learned: Publishing requires custom styling for each output format.

Optimizing Output Configurations: What I Learned the Hard Way

When I first started publishing with DITA, I didn't realize how much control I had over customizing output formatting. If you don't configure outputs properly, you end up with basic-looking documents that don't reflect branding or usability needs.

Here's what I wish I knew earlier:

>>Optimize CSS for Responsive HTML Outputs – Web documentation should be mobile-friendly.
 >>Customize PDF Layouts – Use XSL-FO templates to control headers, footers, and page styling.
 >>Enable Conditional Processing – Filter content dynamically for different audiences, product versions, or platforms.

>>Automate Publishing for Large-Scale Documentation – Set up CI/CD workflows for continuous publishing.

Example: Applying Branding Styles in HTML Output

When I needed to apply a custom company theme, I used a custom CSS file in my DITA-OT configuration:

```
<stylesheet href="company-theme.css"/>
```

✓ This ensured all HTML outputs used my company's branded fonts, colors, and styles.

Troubleshooting Common Publishing Issues

If there's one thing I've learned, it's this: DITA publishing rarely works perfectly the first time.

Here are the most common issues I faced—and how to fix them:

✘ Issue: Images not appearing in PDF output
 >>Fix: Ensure that all image references use relative paths, and that high-resolution images are embedded correctly.

✘ Issue: Tables or lists breaking in HTML5
 >>Fix: Modify CSS styles to ensure proper rendering of lists and tables.

✘ Issue: Slow processing times for large documentation sets
 >>Fix: Use incremental builds to process only modified files instead of regenerating everything.

✘ Issue: Content missing from certain outputs
 >>Fix: Check DITA-OT logs to ensure there are no filtering conflicts or missing dependencies.

Early in my DITA journey, I wasted hours trying to debug why a table wouldn't appear in my HTML output—only to realize that I had a typo in my CSS class name.

✓ Lesson learned: Always check the processing logs for errors before troubleshooting formatting manually.

Looking back, DITA publishing seemed overwhelming at first, but once I understood how each step works, it became a powerful tool.

>>Publishing is more than just generating files—it's about controlling styling, structure, and automation.
 >>Each output format (HTML, PDF, ePub, etc.) has unique formatting challenges.
 >>Troubleshooting is part of the publishing process—expect errors, but learn how to fix them efficiently.

Now that we've covered how DITA content is transformed and published, the next section will explore enterprise-level content management—how DITA integrates with CMS platforms, handles multi-user collaboration, and scales for large organizations.

Advanced Publishing Workflows for Enterprises

Publishing at an enterprise level is a different challenge altogether. It's no longer just about generating PDFs or HTML files—it's about automating, scaling, localizing, and ensuring consistency across multiple teams and product versions.

Many large organizations handle thousands of DITA topics spread across different teams, departments, and languages. This means documentation must be:

>>Updated continuously to match product releases.
 >>Processed automatically instead of relying on manual publishing.

\>>Structured for localization, so translations remain synchronized.
\>>Optimized for performance, ensuring that massive documentation repositories don't slow down publishing pipelines.

Enterprise teams don't just publish documentation—they run content operations at scale. This section will cover:

✓ How organizations automate documentation publishing using CI/CD pipelines.
✓ How DITA integrates with enterprise CMS platforms.
✓ How global companies manage multi-language documentation at scale.
✓ How to optimize performance when handling massive documentation repositories.
✓ How to create custom publishing pipelines tailored to enterprise needs.

Automating Documentation Delivery with CI/CD Pipelines

Why Automation is Essential for Enterprise Publishing?

In a small-scale setup, a technical writer may run DITA-OT manually to generate documentation when needed. But at an enterprise level, where dozens of contributors are making updates daily, publishing workflows must be automated to ensure efficiency, version control, and accuracy.

\>>Manual publishing doesn't scale when documentation updates happen frequently.
\>>CI/CD (Continuous Integration/Continuous Deployment) pipelines automate documentation processing.
\>>Error checking, formatting validation, and publishing can be handled in a single automated workflow.

How CI/CD Works for Documentation?

A CI/CD pipeline detects changes, processes documentation, and automatically deploys the output.

Example workflow:

1. A writer updates content in a DITA repository (e.g., GitHub, Bitbucket).
2. A CI/CD tool (like Jenkins, GitHub Actions) triggers a build process.
3. DITA-OT runs automatically to generate HTML, PDF, or other output formats.
4. Automated quality checks validate broken links, missing topics, and formatting issues.
5. Final output is published to a documentation website, CMS, or customer portal.

Example: A GitHub Actions Pipeline for DITA-OT

```yaml
name: Build and Deploy DITA Docs
on:
  push:
    branches:
      - main
jobs:
  build:
    runs-on: ubuntu-latest
    steps:
      - name: Checkout Repository
        uses: actions/checkout@v3
      - name: Install DITA-OT
        run: curl -L
https://dita-ot.org/download/latest.zip -o dita-ot.zip
&& unzip dita-ot.zip
      - name: Run DITA Build
        run: dita-ot/bin/dita -i docs.ditamap -f html5
      - name: Deploy Docs
        run: rsync -avz output/
user@server:/var/www/docs
```

Integrating DITA into Large-Scale CMS and Publishing Platforms

At an enterprise level, documentation is often stored in large-scale CMS platforms instead of local files. A DITA-enabled CMS allows:

>>Multiple authors to work collaboratively on structured content.
 >>Version-controlled publishing, ensuring that previous documentation remains intact.
 >>Integration with customer portals, APIs, and enterprise knowledge bases.

Examples of DITA-Compatible CMS Platforms:

CMS Platform	Best For
Paligo	Cloud-based structured content management
IXIASOFT CCMS	Large teams with version control needs
Adobe Experience Manager (AEM)	Enterprise publishing & branding consistency

<table>
<tr><td>DITAworks</td><td>End-to-end structured content workflows</td></tr>
</table>

Example: How an Enterprise CMS Integrates with DITA

1. Writers create structured DITA content within the CMS.
2. The CMS applies metadata, versioning, and workflow approvals.
3. DITA-OT is triggered within the CMS to generate final output.
4. Content is published directly to a web portal, mobile app, or knowledge base.

>>This approach centralizes content creation, avoids duplication, and ensures consistency.

Localization and Translation Workflows for Global Documentation

Enterprise documentation isn't just written in one language—it's often translated into dozens. However, manual translation workflows are inefficient, leading to delays, inconsistencies, and higher costs.

Key Challenges in Localization

✘ Content constantly changes, making it difficult to keep translations synchronized.
✘ Manual translation increases errors and inconsistency across different languages.
✘ Some product versions require different levels of localization.

Best Practices for Automating Localization in DITA

>>Use the `<translate>` attribute to mark content for translation.
>>Leverage key references (`<keyref>`) for dynamic terminology updates.
>>Integrate with Translation Management Systems (TMS) like SDL Trados, Smartling, or Phrase for automated translation workflows.

Example: How DITA Handles Multi-Language Variants

```
<p audience="en-US">Welcome to the documentation.</p>
<p audience="fr-FR">Bienvenue dans la
documentation.</p>
```

>>DITA automatically selects the correct version based on user locale settings.

Performance Optimization: Handling Large Documentation Repositories

When dealing with enterprise-scale documentation, performance becomes a bottleneck. As documentation grows to thousands of topics, processing times can slow down, and searches within the CMS can become inefficient.

Common Bottlenecks and Fixes

As documentation grows from hundreds to thousands of topics, publishing workflows start slowing down, making it difficult for large organizations to maintain efficiency.

In small-scale projects, generating a single HTML or PDF output might take just a few seconds. But in enterprise environments, where thousands of files need processing, a single build can take hours if not properly optimized.

Through trial and error, I've seen some of the biggest bottlenecks that slow down enterprise DITA workflows—and more importantly, I've learned how to fix them.

✘ Slow Build Times: Processing Takes Too Long

The Problem:
When working with massive documentation repositories, running DITA-OT builds can become painfully slow. Every time a build is triggered, DITA-OT processes all files from scratch, even if only a small portion of the content has changed.

In enterprise setups, where documentation updates happen daily, waiting hours for builds is not an option.

The Fix:
To solve this, organizations implement incremental builds—instead of regenerating the entire documentation set, only modified files are processed.

Enabling Incremental Builds in DITA-OT:

```
dita -i large-docs.ditamap -f pdf
-Dargs.incremental=true
```

This tells DITA-OT to skip unchanged files, reducing build times by up to 70%.

✗ Slow Search Performance in a CMS

The Problem:
In a DITA-enabled CMS, search performance is critical. As documentation scales, searching across thousands of topics can take several seconds or even minutes—which is unacceptable in fast-paced enterprise environments.

Slow searches happen because:
>>The CMS doesn't pre-index content, forcing it to scan the entire database.
>>Metadata and key-based referencing aren't optimized, making queries inefficient.
>>Some content is duplicated, increasing database size and query load.

The Fix:
>>Implement pre-indexing to ensure search queries return results instantly.
>>Optimize metadata tagging to help the CMS filter content faster.
>>Use key references (`<keyref>`) to dynamically resolve content without duplication.

Many enterprise DITA CMS platforms (like IXIASOFT CCMS or Adobe AEM) support pre-indexing, ensuring that search performance remains fast, even for massive documentation sets.

✗ Large File Sizes in PDFs: Unoptimized Content

The Problem:
Enterprise documentation often includes:
>>High-resolution images
>>Complex tables with multiple columns
>>Embedded fonts for branding

All of these increase file sizes, leading to:
✗ Slow PDF rendering

✘ Increased storage and bandwidth usage
✘ Longer download times for users

The Fix:

>>Optimize images by converting them to compressed formats (WebP, optimized PNGs).

>>Use table formatting best practices to reduce unnecessary data in large tables.

>>Embed only essential fonts—instead of including multiple font families, define primary and secondary typefaces.

Example: Image Optimization for PDF Publishing

```
<image href="diagram.webp" width="600px"/>
```

>>Switching from PNG to WebP reduces image sizes by up to 80% without losing quality.

When dealing with enterprise documentation at scale, performance optimization is not optional—it's a necessity.

>>Incremental builds speed up processing times for large documentation sets.

>>CMS pre-indexing ensures fast search performance across thousands of topics.

>>Optimized images, tables, and fonts improve PDF generation speed and usability.

A well-optimized publishing pipeline ensures that enterprise documentation remains efficient, scalable, and accessible—regardless of size.

Custom Publishing Pipelines: Tailoring DITA-OT for Enterprise Needs

Standard DITA-OT publishing works for most cases, but enterprises often need customization to:

>>Apply branded styling, typography, and layouts.
>>Integrate structured content with other platforms.
>>Generate specialized reports and analytics.

Example: Automating Publishing with Python

```
import os
os.system("dita -i docs.ditamap -f html5")
os.system("scp output/* server:/var/www/docs")
```

>>This script automates processing and deployment in one step.

Enterprise publishing requires far more than just running DITA-OT. Organizations need:

>>CI/CD pipelines to automate documentation delivery.
>>CMS integrations for multi-author collaboration and content management.
>>Localization workflows to maintain consistency across multiple languages.
>>Performance optimization to handle massive documentation repositories.
>>Custom pipelines to meet unique enterprise publishing needs.

With these strategies, DITA can scale from a small documentation project to a fully automated enterprise content system. Now, let's move on to DITA localization and multilingual support—how organizations handle global documentation across multiple languages, cultures, and regulatory requirements.

Chapter 5

DITA Style Guide

When working with structured content, one of the biggest challenges isn't just writing the content—it's writing it consistently. I learned this the hard way.

Early in my DITA journey, I was part of a project where multiple writers contributed to the same documentation set. Everyone followed the same structured authoring principles—Concepts, Tasks, and References were in place, metadata was assigned, and conditional processing was correctly applied. But something still felt off.

The documentation lacked uniformity in style, terminology, and structure. One writer would say, *"Click the Save button,"* while another would write, *"Press Save."* Some sections were overly detailed, while others were too concise. UI elements were inconsistently formatted, and certain documents sounded conversational, while others read like legal contracts.

That's when I realized that a structured content model alone doesn't guarantee clarity—it must be backed by a clear, well-defined style guide that ensures all documentation follows consistent writing, terminology, and formatting standards.

A DITA Style Guide is more than a set of writing rules—it's a framework that:

>>Maintains consistency across large teams
>>Improves content readability and usability
>>Enhances reusability and scalability
>>Optimizes content for localization and automation

This chapter is about that missing piece—the DITA Style Guide—and how it transforms structured content into a cohesive, standardized, and scalable documentation system.

Why Style Guides Matter in Structured Content

A style guide is often overlooked when people start with structured authoring. Writers focus on XML rules, tagging conventions, and metadata—but they often forget that structured content needs to be consistent in writing style, tone, and formatting just as much as it needs to be technically accurate.

I've seen teams struggle with:

- Inconsistent terminology (*Are we calling it a "screen" or a "window"?*)
- Varying sentence structures (*Click Save? Press Save? Select the Save button?*)
- Unclear organization of concepts and instructions
- Repetitive or redundant content caused by a lack of reusability guidelines

In DITA, content is not linear—it's modular. A single topic may be reused across multiple outputs, meaning even small inconsistencies amplify over time.

A DITA Style Guide standardizes:

>>How topics are structured (Concept, Task, Reference, etc.)
 >>How sentences are written (Active voice? Direct instructions?)

>>How UI elements, commands, and links are formatted
>>How metadata is used to improve searchability and classification

Without a style guide, DITA content quickly becomes chaotic, making maintenance a nightmare.

What Makes a DITA Style Guide Different?

Before working with DITA, I had used traditional style guides like the Microsoft Writing Style Guide and the Chicago Manual of Style. These guides focus on:

>>Grammar rules
>>Punctuation, sentence structure, and voice
>>Formatting (bold, italics, headings)

But when I started working in DITA, I realized that traditional style guides alone don't work.

A DITA Style Guide is different because it must account for structured content principles:

Aspect	Traditional Style Guide	DITA-Specific Style Guide
Sentence Structure	Encourages clear, concise writing	Defines sentence structure based on topic types (Concept, Task, Reference)
Terminology	Standardizes industry terms	Uses metadata-driven taxonomy for term consistency

Formatting	Covers bold, italics, and headings	Dictates XML tagging, metadata, and conditional processing
Document Structure	Focuses on narrative flow	Requires modular, reusable content organization

One of the biggest shifts I had to make was realizing that content in DITA isn't just written—it's engineered. A DITA Style Guide doesn't just focus on how text appears but also how it functions across multiple outputs and reuses.

Key Components of a DITA-Specific Writing Guide

I've worked with companies that have hundreds of writers, all contributing to a single content repository. In those environments, a DITA Style Guide isn't optional—it's a necessity. Here's what a good style guide must include:

1. Writing Standards and Readability Rules

>>Should sentences be in active or passive voice?
>>Should we use imperative instructions (*"Click Save"*) or full sentences (*"To save your changes, click Save"*)?
>>How do we refer to UI elements (buttons, menus, checkboxes)?

Having a style guide eliminates inconsistencies in tone and phrasing, keeping content uniform across thousands of topics.

2. Topic Organization Rules

>>When do we use a Concept, Task, or Reference topic?
>>How do we name topics and structure maps?
>>Should topics be self-contained or cross-referenced?

In traditional writing, we naturally structure content in a linear way. But in DITA, we need to think in modules—and a style guide ensures writers don't fall back into old habits.

3. Metadata and Terminology Management

>>What metadata fields should be mandatory?
>>How do we standardize terminology across multiple teams and departments?
>>How do we define controlled vocabulary for key terms?

Metadata in DITA is more than just search tags—it dictates how content is filtered, reused, and repurposed. A style guide ensures consistent tagging and classification.

4. Reusability and Conditional Processing Rules

>>When do we use Keyrefs, Conrefs, and Reusable Components?
>>How do we structure content for multi-product documentation?
>>What rules should govern conditional processing?

Without clear reusability rules, teams risk duplicating content unnecessarily, leading to maintenance issues. A style guide helps enforce modular, structured authoring principles.

Why Style Guides is a must Need in Large-Scale Documentation?

When working solo or in small teams, style consistency is easy to manage informally. But when documentation scales—across multiple teams, regions, and languages—a well-defined style guide is essential.

In large enterprises, a DITA Style Guide helps:

>>Onboard new writers quickly—they don't have to guess how content should be written.
>>Ensure consistency across thousands of topics—even if dozens of authors are contributing.
>>Improve translation efficiency—consistent phrasing reduces translation costs.
>>Reduce content maintenance overhead—avoids inconsistencies that require frequent revisions.

The biggest mistake I made early in my DITA journey was assuming structure alone was enough. But I quickly realized that structured content without a style guide leads to inconsistency, inefficiency, and poor user experience.

A DITA Style Guide is more than just a reference document—it's a critical framework that shapes how content is written, managed, and maintained.

Now that we understand why a DITA Style Guide is important, the next step is to define its structure, key writing principles, and enforcement strategies. Let's move forward and build a comprehensive, scalable writing framework that works for teams of any size.

Structuring a DITA Style Guide: Key Writing Standards

A DITA Style Guide is only as useful as its structure—if it's too complex, writers won't follow it; if it's too vague, it won't enforce consistency.

When I first tried to create a style guide for a DITA-based documentation project, I made the mistake of overloading it with rules. I added every possible writing convention, detailed XML formatting instructions, and exhaustive metadata guidelines. The result? Nobody used it.

I realized that for a DITA Style Guide to be effective, it must be structured, concise, and easy to follow. It should act as a go-to reference for every writer, ensuring that all content follows the same voice, tone, sentence structure, and terminology rules.

This section defines how to structure a DITA Style Guide effectively, ensuring it remains practical, enforceable, and scalable for large teams.

Voice & Tone Guidelines for Technical Documentation

One of the first things a style guide must define is how the content should "sound".

A consistent voice and tone ensures that readers instantly recognize and trust your documentation. In DITA, content is often used across multiple outputs (PDF, HTML, Help Center, API Docs, etc.), meaning that inconsistencies in tone can become highly noticeable.

>>Voice: The overall personality of the documentation (e.g., professional, casual, authoritative).
 >>Tone: The emotional inflection used in different situations (e.g., instructive, reassuring, neutral).

Example Voice & Tone Guidelines for a DITA Style Guide:

- Keep it professional, but approachable. Avoid overly formal language that feels robotic.
- Use a direct, instructive tone. Write with clarity, not fluff.
- Avoid marketing-style exaggeration. Stick to facts—no "cutting-edge" or "game-changing" terminology.
- Be consistent in terminology usage. If one page refers to a "dashboard," don't call it a "control panel" elsewhere.

Best Practice: Define a list of approved terms (e.g., "administrator" vs. "admin") and maintain it as part of the style guide.

Sentence Structure & Readability Rules in DITA

One of the hardest things to enforce in large teams is sentence clarity. Some writers naturally write short, punchy sentences, while others use long, complex structures that can confuse readers.

A DITA Style Guide must provide clear rules for:

>>Sentence length—recommended word count for clarity.
>>Active vs. passive voice—DITA favors direct, active instructions.
>>Punctuation and grammar consistency—avoiding unnecessary complexity.
>>How to handle UI elements, commands, and procedural steps.

Best Practices for Readability in DITA:

1. Use active voice:
   - ✘ *The file should be saved by clicking the Save button.*
   - ✓ *Click the Save button to save the file.*

2. Keep sentences short and direct (15-20 words max).
   - ✘ *When the system encounters an error in processing the request, it will generate an error message that informs the user about the specific issue.*
   - ✓ *If an error occurs, the system displays a message explaining the issue.*

3. Use consistent phrasing for user actions. Define whether to use "Click" vs. "Select" vs. "Press" and enforce it across all documentation.

Best Practice: If possible, use automated readability checkers to ensure that content remains clear, concise, and easy to scan.

Defining Clear and Concise Writing for Structured Content

Clarity is everything in technical documentation. A DITA Style Guide must enforce structured, logical writing that is easy to scan and understand.

Rules for Writing Clear and Concise DITA Content:

>>One idea per sentence. No unnecessary complexity.
>>One instruction per step. If a process has multiple actions, break them into separate steps.
>>No redundant phrases. Avoid filler words like "basically," "very," or "in order to."
>>Use parallel structure. When listing steps, keep the verb tense consistent.

Example of Overcomplicated Writing (Needs Improvement):

"In order to ensure that the installation process is completed correctly, it is highly recommended that the user follows the given steps carefully, ensuring that each action is carried out before proceeding to the next step."

✓ Rewritten for Clarity:
 "Follow these steps to complete the installation successfully."

>>Shorter.
>>Clearer.
>>Easier to follow.

Terminology Management: Maintaining Consistency in Large Teams

One of the biggest risks in large documentation projects is terminology inconsistency. Different writers often use slightly different terms for the same concept—confusing both readers and translators.

A DITA Style Guide should include:

>>A controlled vocabulary (approved terminology list).
 >>Rules for handling product names, acronyms, and technical jargon.
 >>Guidelines for abbreviation usage (e.g., API vs. Application Programming Interface).

Example: Terminology Inconsistencies and Fixes

✘ Inconsistent Terms	✓ Standardized Term (DITA Style Guide)
Login / Log in / Sign in	Sign in
Click Save / Press Save / Select Save	Click Save
API Key / API Token / Access Key	API Key

By defining consistent terminology, you eliminate confusion and ensure documentation remains searchable and reusable.

Using Taxonomies and Metadata to Improve Writing Quality

A DITA Style Guide isn't just about sentences—it's also about structured metadata. Proper use of taxonomies and metadata improves:

>>Searchability—better indexing in content management systems.
 >>Filtering and conditional processing—custom content views for different audiences.
 >>Content reuse—reduces duplication and makes updating easier.

Metadata Best Practices in a DITA Style Guide:

- Define required metadata fields (e.g., `audience`, `platform`, `product version`).
- Standardize how metadata should be applied across topics.
- Create a controlled vocabulary for metadata values (no random tagging).

Example: Standardizing Metadata in DITA Topics

Instead of allowing inconsistent audience metadata, a style guide should enforce predefined values:

✗ Inconsistent Metadata Values	✓ Standardized Values
Beginner / Basic User / Novice	Beginner
Advanced / Expert / Power User	Advanced

Windows / Windows OS / Win	Windows

By enforcing consistent metadata, writers improve searchability and content filtering across large documentation sets.

A DITA Style Guide should be structured for usability—not just as a reference, but as a practical tool that makes writing easier, faster, and more consistent.

>>Define voice, tone, and readability rules.
>>Standardize terminology and metadata usage.
>>Enforce content structure and clarity guidelines.

Without a style guide, DITA content quickly becomes inconsistent, difficult to manage, and harder to scale. In the next section, we'll explore how to apply these writing rules effectively in DITA topics, maps, and structured content workflows.

Applying Style Guide Rules in DITA Content

A style guide is only valuable if it's actually applied. I've seen teams spend weeks crafting detailed style guides, only for writers to completely ignore them because they weren't practical to follow.

In DITA, following a style guide isn't just about writing correctly—it's about structuring content effectively, ensuring metadata consistency, and maintaining modularity. A well-applied style guide helps reduce content duplication, improve searchability, and make localization easier.

This section focuses on how to implement style guide rules practically, ensuring that every piece of DITA content—whether a

Concept, Task, Reference, or Troubleshooting topic—follows a consistent, structured approach.

Standardizing Content Across Different Topic Types

One of the most common mistakes I see in DITA documentation is misusing topic types. Writers often mix instructions inside concept topics or add background explanations in task topics—completely breaking the structured approach.

A DITA Style Guide must define clear rules for when and how to use each topic type:

Best Practices for Using DITA Topic Types

Topic Type	Purpose	Example
Concept	Explains background information, principles, or theory.	*"What is API Rate Limiting?"*
Task	Step-by-step instructions for performing an action.	*"How to Set Up API Rate Limits in the Dashboard"*

Reference	Provides structured information, such as tables, lists, and API parameters.	*"API Rate Limits: Request Limits by Plan Type"*
Troubleshooting	Helps users solve common issues.	*"Fixing API Rate Limit Errors (429 Responses)"*

⇥How to Enforce This in a Style Guide?

\>\>Clearly define which type of content belongs in each topic type.

\>\>Provide real-world examples so writers can see correct vs. incorrect implementations.

\>\>Use Schematron rules to validate that each topic follows its correct structure.

Guidelines for Writing Modular, Reusable Topics

In traditional documentation, writers often repeat the same explanations across multiple documents. In DITA, however, content should be modular and reusable, eliminating unnecessary duplication.

Style Guide Rules for Modular Writing

\>\>Each topic should be self-contained. Avoid relying on context from other topics.

\>\>No redundant information. Instead of copying content, use conrefs (content references) for reuse.

\>\>Write small, focused topics. If a topic addresses multiple user needs, split it into separate topics.

⇥Example: Before vs. After Applying Modular Writing Rules

✘ Before (Traditional Writing)

"To set up API rate limits, navigate to the dashboard, select API settings, and configure the request limit per minute. API rate limiting is a technique used to control the number of requests a user can make to an API in a given time period."

✓ After (DITA Modular Writing)

1. Concept Topic: *"What is API Rate Limiting?"*
2. Task Topic: *"How to Configure API Rate Limits in the Dashboard."*
3. Reference Topic: *"API Rate Limits by Plan Type (Comparison Table)."*

Each topic now serves a single, clear purpose, allowing for better reuse and automation.

Applying Metadata and Keyrefs for Style Enforcement

Metadata Standardization

Metadata isn't just an extra layer of information—it directly impacts searchability, filtering, and conditional processing in DITA.

A style guide must enforce metadata consistency by:
>>Defining mandatory metadata fields (e.g., audience, platform, product version).
>>Standardizing values for filtering and taxonomy.
>>Enforcing consistent use of index terms and categories.

Example: Correct vs. Incorrect Metadata Usage

Topic Type	Incorrect Metadata Usage	Correct Metadata Usage

Conce pt	audience="all" (too broad)	audience="developer"
Task	platform="Windows , Mac, Linux" (inconsistent format)	platform="Windows" platform="Mac" platform="Linux" (separate attributes)
Refere nce	Missing index terms	indexterm="API Limits, Throttling, Rate Limits"

»How to Enforce This in a Style Guide?
 >>Predefine metadata categories so writers select from approved values.
 >>Use CCMS (Component Content Management Systems) to enforce metadata tagging rules.
 >>Validate metadata using Schematron and automated checks.

Handling UI Elements, Variables, and Inline Formatting in DITA

Another common inconsistency in DITA content is how writers refer to UI elements, code snippets, and inline text formatting.

A DITA Style Guide must standardize:

>>Button labels, menu names, and command references.
>>Inline code formatting rules (e.g., <code> tags for syntax).
>>How to handle dynamic content (variables, placeholders, keyrefs).

Best Practices for UI and Inline Formatting in DITA

Element	Incorrect Example	Correct Example (Following DITA Style Guide)
Button Label	*Click on "Save"*	Click Save (No quotes, no "on")
Menu Navigation	*Go to the settings ↠ API settings*	Go to Settings > API Settings
Inline Code	*Enter api_key = "12345"*	Enter `api_key = "12345"`

↠How to Enforce This in a Style Guide?

>>Define approved UI terminology and phrasing rules.

>>Specify formatting conventions for inline text, code snippets, and

dynamic placeholders.
>>Use Schematron rules to flag incorrect formatting in XML content.

Standardizing Captions, Tables, and Lists for Structured Content

Writers often format tables and lists differently, leading to inconsistent visual output. A DITA Style Guide must define:

>>Standard rules for tables (headers, row alignment, formatting).
>>When to use ordered vs. unordered lists.
>>How to write clear, concise captions for images and tables.

Example Table Formatting Rules

Element	Incorrect Formatting	Correct Formatting (DITA Standard)
Table Headings	Missing headers	All tables must have `<thead>` with column names.
List Items	Using bullets for sequences	Use numbered lists for step-by-step actions.
Image Captions	*Figure 1: This is an image.*	`<figdesc> User authentication process overview.</figdesc>`

»How to Enforce This in a Style Guide?
>>Define list formatting standards (when to use numbered vs.
bulleted lists).
>>Set rules for table captions, column formatting, and accessibility.
>>Use automated validation to check table structures before
publishing.

A DITA Style Guide is useless unless it's enforced. I've worked on
projects where writers had the right documentation guidelines but
didn't follow them, leading to inconsistent, hard-to-maintain content.

By applying style guide rules in topic types, metadata, UI references,
and structured elements, documentation teams can ensure:
>>Clarity and readability across all outputs.
>>Easier content reuse and automation.
>>A structured, scalable documentation system that remains
consistent over time.

Enforcing the DITA Style Guide at Scale

Creating a DITA Style Guide is one thing—getting people to follow it
consistently is another. In smaller teams, enforcing a style guide
might be as simple as asking writers to read it and apply the rules. But
in large enterprises, where hundreds of writers contribute to
documentation across multiple products, manual enforcement
becomes impractical.

Unlike traditional documentation workflows—where editors manually
check for inconsistencies—DITA allows automated validation and
governance using tools like Schematron, DITA-OT customizations,
and Component Content Management Systems (CCMS).

This section covers how to implement governance strategies and
automate style enforcement, ensuring that all DITA-based content
follows consistent writing, formatting, and structural rules at scale.

How Large Enterprises Implement Style Guide Governance

In a large-scale DITA environment, enforcing a style guide requires a structured governance framework. Large organizations rely on three key governance strategies:

1. Style Guide Documentation & Training

>>Every writer, editor, and reviewer must have access to the DITA Style Guide.
 >>Style rules should be documented in a structured, easy-to-navigate format (not buried in PDFs or wikis).
 >>Teams should conduct periodic training sessions to keep all contributors aligned.

Example: How IBM Implements Style Governance
 »IBM's DITA documentation teams use an internal writing guide, accessible within their Component Content Management System (CCMS).
 »Writers undergo structured onboarding training to learn topic-based authoring principles and terminology rules.
 »The CCMS enforces metadata tagging and structure validation, ensuring compliance before content reaches review.

2. Automated Validation & Error Detection

>>Manual reviews are inefficient for large-scale content operations.
 >>Enterprises use automated validation tools to flag style violations in real time.
 >>Schematron and DITA-OT custom rules help detect errors before content is published.

Example: Adobe's DITA Workflow
 »Adobe's tech writing teams use automated XML validation scripts to check content against predefined style rules.
 »If an article fails validation, the system blocks publication until the

issues are resolved.

→This ensures consistent, high-quality documentation across their product ecosystem.

Using Schematron and Automated Validation to Enforce Style Rules

Schematron is an XML-based rule-checking language that allows teams to validate structured content against predefined style rules. Unlike DTDs or XML schemas, Schematron can check for complex style inconsistencies—ensuring that content adheres to the DITA Style Guide.

How Schematron Enforces Style Rules in DITA

>>Detects structural inconsistencies (e.g., a Concept topic containing step-by-step instructions).

>>Validates metadata usage (e.g., ensuring all Task topics include `audience="developer"`).

>>Flags inconsistent UI references (e.g., using *"press OK"* instead of *"click OK"*).

Example Schematron Rule for Enforcing Task Topic Structure

```
<rule context="task">
    <assert test="steps">
        ERROR: A Task topic must contain <steps>.
    </assert>
</rule>
```

→If a Task topic lacks `<steps>`, this rule flags an error, preventing the content from being published until it is corrected.

Best Practice: Enterprises integrate Schematron validation into their CI/CD documentation pipelines, automatically checking for style violations whenever new content is added.

Customizing DITA-OT to Flag Style Violations

DITA Open Toolkit (DITA-OT) is a powerful publishing engine, but its default configuration doesn't enforce writing style rules. To ensure style guide compliance, organizations customize DITA-OT processing scripts to flag errors automatically.

How Custom DITA-OT Processing Can Enforce Style Rules

>>Generate error reports if writing style rules are violated.
>>Modify DITA-OT transformations to flag inconsistencies.
>>Automatically insert warnings in output files (e.g., PDFs, HTML) if violations exist.

Example: How SAP Uses Custom DITA-OT Rules
»SAP's technical documentation team customized their DITA-OT pipeline to detect formatting inconsistencies in UI references and inline text.
»If a violation occurs, the build process displays a warning and provides a link to the DITA Style Guide for correction.

Automated Review Workflows: Catching Style Errors Before Publishing

A manual review process is not scalable in large enterprises. Instead, organizations implement automated review workflows, ensuring that style violations are caught before content reaches the end-user.

Best Practices for Automating Style Reviews in DITA

>>Pre-publication validation: Automatically scan content for style violations before publishing.
>>Continuous style compliance: Regularly audit existing content repositories to identify outdated or inconsistent documentation.
>>Integration with authoring tools: Use CCMS plugins to flag errors while writers are creating content (before submission).

Example: Microsoft's DITA Style Review Process
»Microsoft integrates DITA validation tools into their CCMS, flagging inconsistent sentence structures, terminology mismatches, and UI inconsistencies in real time.
»Editors receive automated reports highlighting issues, ensuring style compliance before content is released.

Integrating the Style Guide with a CCMS

For enterprises with thousands of DITA topics, enforcing a style guide manually is impossible. This is where Component Content Management Systems (CCMS) play a crucial role.

A CCMS enforces DITA style rules by:

>>Automatically applying metadata and tagging rules.
>>Validating topic structures and checking for missing required elements.
>>Flagging inconsistent terminology and enforcing approved style guidelines.
>>Managing version control and approval workflows to prevent undocumented changes.

Example: How Oracle Uses a CCMS for Style Enforcement
↠Oracle's CCMS enforces metadata consistency by requiring all Reference topics to include index terms.
↠Writers receive real-time feedback while editing, preventing style guide violations before submission.

Without automation and governance, even the most well-designed DITA Style Guide will fail at scale.

>>Schematron rules ensure structural and metadata consistency.
>>Custom DITA-OT processing flags style violations automatically.
>>CCMS integration ensures real-time enforcement within authoring workflows.

By combining these automated validation techniques, enterprises can maintain content consistency across thousands of topics, ensuring that every piece of documentation follows the DITA Style Guide—without relying on slow, manual review processes.

In the next section, we'll explore how to evolve and maintain a DITA Style Guide over time, ensuring it stays relevant as products, teams, and content requirements change.

Evolving and Maintaining a DITA Style Guide

Creating a DITA Style Guide is not a one-time effort—it's a living document that must evolve with the organization, industry standards, and technology trends.

Early in my career, I assumed that once a style guide was written, it was set in stone—something that writers could reference indefinitely. But I quickly realized that language changes, tools evolve, and business needs shift.

What worked five years ago in software documentation might be outdated today due to API-driven documentation trends. What was once a simple set of rules might become a rigid constraint that no longer fits how teams work.

A static style guide quickly becomes irrelevant. This section is about how to keep it dynamic, scalable, and useful—ensuring that it continuously serves writers, editors, and content strategists in an ever-changing documentation landscape.

How to Continuously Improve a DITA Style Guide

The 3 Pillars of a Maintainable Style Guide:

1. Regular Audits » Keep the guide updated and relevant.
2. Feedback Loops » Ensure writers actively contribute to improving it.
3. Scalability » Structure the guide so that it remains usable as teams grow.

Regular Audits: Keeping the Guide Relevant

A style guide isn't meant to sit on a shelf—it must be reviewed and updated periodically to keep up with:

>>New documentation trends (e.g., AI-generated content, voice interfaces, API doc changes).
>>Evolving DITA standards (e.g., changes in metadata handling or specialization).
>>Shifts in company branding and terminology.

How Often Should You Review the Style Guide?

- Quarterly ↠ Small revisions (terminology changes, minor updates).
- Annually ↠ Major revisions (new writing principles, emerging best practices).

↠Best Practice: Assign a dedicated governance team responsible for maintaining the guide. This could include senior writers, content strategists, and DITA architects.

Feedback Loops: Encouraging Contributor Input

A style guide should serve the writing team, not feel like an imposed rulebook. One mistake I made early on was treating the guide as something only I could modify—this led to frustration among writers who had valuable insights but no way to contribute.

>>Create an open feedback system ↠ Writers should be able to submit change requests or suggest improvements.
>>Hold periodic discussions ↠ Invite technical writers, information architects, and editors to review the guide together.
>>Use surveys ↠ Gather feedback on which style rules help or hinder efficiency.

Best Practice: Maintain a "proposed changes" section where pending updates are tracked before approval.

Scalability: Structuring the Guide for Growth

As documentation scales, a style guide should be easy to navigate—nobody has time to sift through long PDFs or outdated Word documents.

>>Use a structured, modular format (just like DITA content).
>>Organize by categories:

- Writing Style ↦ Sentence structure, tone, voice
- Metadata & Taxonomy ↦ Controlled vocabulary, indexing
- Topic Organization ↦ Concept, Task, Reference
- UI Formatting Rules ↦ Buttons, commands, syntax

Example: Adobe maintains its DITA style guide as a web-based, searchable document within its CCMS, ensuring quick updates and easy access.

Versioning the Style Guide for Consistency Over Time

As content teams grow, different versions of the style guide might circulate across teams—leading to inconsistencies.

Versioning solves this problem by ensuring that all contributors are using the most recent version while still retaining access to historical versions.

How to Version a DITA Style Guide?

>>Assign version numbers (e.g., Style Guide v1.2, v1.3).
>>Keep a changelog ↦ Document what's changed in each version.
>>Archive older versions ↦ Writers can reference previous rules if needed.
>>Communicate updates clearly ↦ Notify all writers whenever the guide is updated.

↦Best Practice: Use CCMS version control to automatically track changes, ensuring that updates don't overwrite important guidelines.

Adapting Style Rules for New Technologies and Industries

I've worked with teams where a style guide was perfect for traditional user manuals but fell apart when applied to API documentation.

The reality is that different types of content require different style considerations.

>>API documentation ⇥ Requires strict terminology standardization (e.g., "parameter" vs. "argument").
>>Chatbot/AI-generated content ⇥ May require conversational tone rules.
>>Regulated industries (healthcare, finance, etc.) ⇥ Must align with legal documentation standards.

Best Practice: Maintain industry-specific style guide extensions—so that specialized teams can follow the core DITA guidelines but adapt them for their use case.

Handling Contributor Training and Onboarding

Even the best DITA Style Guide is useless if new writers don't know how to use it.

How to Onboard New Writers to a DITA Style Guide:

>>Provide interactive training ⇥ Conduct onboarding sessions for all new writers.
>>Use real-world examples ⇥ Show correct vs. incorrect implementations.
>>Make the guide searchable ⇥ Ensure new contributors can quickly find answers.

>>Assign mentors » Pair new writers with experienced team members to guide them.

»Best Practice: Create short video tutorials or microlearning sessions to introduce key style guide rules.

Case Study: How IBM Maintains Its DITA Style Guide

IBM has one of the most comprehensive DITA-based documentation ecosystems—managing thousands of topics across multiple teams.

Here's how they maintain their DITA Style Guide at scale:

»Governance Team: A dedicated team of content strategists and DITA experts manages the guide.
»Automated Enforcement: IBM integrates Schematron validation into their CCMS, flagging style violations before content is published.
»Quarterly Updates: The guide is updated every 3 months based on team feedback and industry trends.
»Version Control: Every new version is archived and logged, ensuring consistency.
»Training & Compliance: All new writers must complete a style guide training before contributing.

Key Takeaway: IBM's structured approach ensures that even with a large, distributed team, their DITA documentation remains consistent, clear, and compliant.

A DITA Style Guide is never finished—it must evolve to remain useful.

>>Regular audits ensure it stays relevant.
>>Versioning prevents confusion across teams.
>>Adapting to new technologies keeps documentation up to date.
>>Ongoing training ensures that all writers follow the guidelines.

A style guide is only valuable if it's actively maintained and used. By following these strategies, organizations can ensure that their DITA documentation remains structured, scalable, and future-proof.

Styling and Visual Consistency in DITA Outputs

While DITA excels at structuring content, it does not control presentation—this is where CSS, XSL-FO, and theming strategies come into play. Without proper styling rules, DITA outputs can look inconsistent across platforms (HTML, PDF, ePub, WebHelp).

I've seen documentation projects where writing standards were perfectly followed, but the final outputs looked chaotic—inconsistent fonts, mismatched colors, and unreadable PDFs. That's why a well-defined styling strategy is crucial in any DITA Style Guide.

This section explains how to enforce visual consistency across different DITA outputs, ensuring a unified, branded, and accessible presentation for all documentation.

How CSS Works in DITA Outputs?

By default, DITA does not handle styling—instead, CSS (for HTML) and XSL-FO (for PDF) control the final look of published content.

Key Points About CSS in DITA Outputs:

>>CSS applies only to web-based outputs (HTML, WebHelp, ePub, etc.).
>>PDF styling requires XSL-FO or custom DITA-OT plugins.
>>CSS can be reused across multiple deliverables for a consistent look.

Example: Attaching a CSS File to DITA Outputs

To apply CSS to a DITA-generated HTML output, you must:

1. Define a CSS file with style rules.

2. Reference it inside a DITA-OT transformation.

3. Ensure selectors match the DITA-generated HTML elements.

>>Example CSS File (`dita-style.css`)

```css
body {
   font-family: Arial, sans-serif;
   line-height: 1.6;
   color: #333;
}

h1, h2, h3 {
   font-weight: bold;
   color: #005A9C;
}

code {
   background-color: #f4f4f4;
   font-family: monospace;
   padding: 4px;
   border-radius: 3px;
}
```

Applying the CSS to DITA HTML Output (in `args.css` configuration):

```xml
<property name="args.css" value="dita-style.css"/>
```

This ensures that all HTML-based outputs follow the same typography, colors, and spacing, providing consistent branding across all web deliverables.

Standardizing Typography, Colors, and Layout

One of the biggest issues in DITA styling is inconsistent typography and colors—without proper standardization, different teams might use different fonts, inconsistent line spacing, or mismatched color schemes.

Best Practices for Standardized Typography and Layout:

>>Use a defined font stack (e.g., `Arial, sans-serif` for modern UIs, `Times New Roman` for print).
>>Set clear rules for heading sizes (H1, H2, H3).
>>Define color schemes to match branding guidelines.
>>Maintain consistent margins, padding, and whitespace for readability.

Here is example of Enforcing Font and Color Consistency in DITA CSS

```css
:root {
  --primary-color: #005A9C;
  --secondary-color: #0078D4;
  --text-color: #333;
}

/* Apply typography */
body {
  font-family: 'Roboto', sans-serif;
  color: var(--text-color);
  font-size: 16px;
}

/* Standardized headings */
h1 {
  font-size: 28px;
  color: var(--primary-color);
}

h2 {
  font-size: 24px;
  color: var(--secondary-color);
```

```
}

h3 {
  font-size: 20px;
  color: var(--secondary-color);
}
```

»Best Practice: Maintain a single CSS file per brand/product, ensuring consistency across all documentation teams.

Applying CSS and XSL-FO for PDF, HTML, and WebHelp

DITA-generated PDFs require different styling rules than web-based outputs.

- CSS controls HTML/WebHelp styling.
- XSL-FO controls PDF layouts, fonts, and pagination.

How to Define XSL-FO Styles for PDF Output

Unlike CSS, XSL-FO uses XML-based rules to define PDF structure, page size, margins, and fonts.

>>Example XSL-FO Rule for Controlling Page Layout in PDFs

```
<fo:layout-master-set>
    <fo:simple-page-master master-name="A4"
page-height="29.7cm" page-width="21cm" margin="2cm">
        <fo:region-body margin-top="2cm"
margin-bottom="2cm"/>
        <fo:region-before extent="1cm"/>
        <fo:region-after extent="1cm"/>
    </fo:simple-page-master>
</fo:layout-master-set>
```

⇥Best Practice: Use predefined templates for XSL-FO to ensure consistent PDF formatting across multiple documentation deliverables.

Ensuring Accessibility and Readability in Structured Content

A DITA Style Guide must include accessibility rules to ensure compliance with WCAG (Web Content Accessibility Guidelines) and other accessibility standards.

Key Accessibility Best Practices for DITA Outputs:

>>Use semantic HTML for web outputs (avoid `<div>`-only layouts).
>>Ensure proper heading structure (H1 ⇥ H2 ⇥ H3, no skips).
>>Define accessible contrast ratios for text and background colors.
>>Include ARIA roles for assistive technologies.

Example: Applying Accessible Color Contrast Rules in CSS

```css
body {
   color: #333;
   background-color: #fff;
}

/* Ensure links are readable */
a {
   color: #005A9C;
}

a:hover {
   color: #002F5A;
}
```

⇥Best Practice: Use contrast checkers to validate readability across all devices.

Customizing Branding for Enterprise Documentation

Enterprise organizations often require custom branding for different products or teams, meaning DITA content must be themed dynamically.

Best Practices for Branding DITA Outputs:

>>Use CSS variables for color theming.
>>Allow dynamic switching of stylesheets per brand.
>>Ensure logos, icons, and UI components are consistent across products.

Example: Using CSS Variables for Multi-Brand Documentation

```css
/* Default brand theme */
:root {
   --brand-primary: #005A9C;
   --brand-secondary: #0078D4;
}

/* Alternate theme for a different product */
[data-brand="productX"] {
   --brand-primary: #E63946;
   --brand-secondary: #F4A261;
}

/* Apply branding */
h1 {
   color: var(--brand-primary);
}

h2 {
   color: var(--brand-secondary);
}
```

⇢Best Practice: Use metadata-driven theming, so the correct CSS file is applied based on product name, audience, or region.

A DITA Style Guide is incomplete without visual consistency rules. By enforcing CSS/XSL-FO guidelines, teams can ensure:

>>Readable, accessible, and well-structured outputs.
>>Consistent branding across web, PDF, and mobile documentation.
>>Scalability—so all future documentation matches the company's look and feel.

Without proper styling rules, structured content can still look unstructured. A well-designed DITA styling framework ensures that writing standards don't just exist in XML—they're reflected in every published document.

Chapter 6

DITA in Action

We've covered how DITA works, but how do real companies use it in their day-to-day documentation workflows? This chapter goes beyond theory—exploring how industries like software, healthcare, finance, and manufacturing leverage DITA for scalable, structured content. We'll also look at how Agile teams integrate DITA with DevOps, and what the future of structured authoring looks like with AI, automation, and headless CMS platforms.

DITA in Industry-Specific Documentation

When I first started working with DITA, I saw it as an abstract, technical framework—structured, logical, and efficient. But what really solidified my understanding was seeing how it's used in real-world industries, solving actual documentation challenges at scale.

For many organizations, documentation isn't just about writing—it's about compliance, automation, and content reuse across thousands of deliverables. Whether it's API docs at IBM, regulatory filings in healthcare, financial compliance reports, or manufacturing manuals,

DITA is the backbone of structured content in industries that demand consistency, scalability, and efficiency.

Let's walk through how leading companies in different sectors use DITA, not just as a documentation tool, but as a critical part of their content infrastructure.

Software Documentation & API Writing

How IBM, Google, and Microsoft Use DITA for API Documentation?

I remember the first time I saw an enterprise API documentation workflow—it was nothing like the typical Markdown-based API guides I had worked with before. Companies like IBM, Google, and Microsoft aren't just writing documentation; they're building massive, scalable documentation ecosystems where APIs, SDKs, and user manuals must be automatically generated, version-controlled, and localized.

↠IBM Developer Docs ↠ IBM uses DITA to create API documentation that integrates with their automated CI/CD workflows. Instead of manually writing API reference guides, IBM's engineers define API specifications, and DITA processes them into structured outputs—PDFs, HTML5, and developer portals.

↠Google Cloud Docs ↠ Google takes a hybrid approach—DITA manages their structured content, while API specs are stored in Swagger/OpenAPI formats, ensuring real-time updates. The key is content modularity—API descriptions, error messages, and usage guidelines exist as reusable DITA topics, meaning they don't need to be rewritten across multiple products.

↠Microsoft Developer Network (MSDN) ↠ Microsoft's documentation scales across thousands of APIs. Using DITA specializations for technical writing, they maintain consistency in API call descriptions, example responses, and metadata, ensuring that developers always get accurate, versioned information.

Lesson Learned:
DITA isn't just for user guides—it's a core part of API documentation workflows, where automation, reusability, and structured content play a huge role in scaling tech documentation.

Healthcare and Medical Compliance Documentation

How Siemens Healthineers and FDA-Regulated Organizations Use DITA

In industries like healthcare, medical devices, and pharmaceuticals, documentation isn't just helpful—it's legally required.

I once worked with a team dealing with medical device documentation, and I quickly realized something: Every sentence, every warning label, and every procedure must be approved for compliance. A single documentation mistake could mean regulatory violations, product recalls, or even legal risks.

That's where DITA steps in, enabling traceability, version control, and compliance-driven workflows.

↠Siemens Healthineers ↠ Siemens uses DITA to manage medical documentation across multiple languages. Their product manuals must be 100% consistent across regions, following strict European MDR (Medical Device Regulation) and FDA guidelines.

↠FDA-Regulated Medical Device Documentation ↠ In the U.S., any medical device content must follow FDA 21 CFR Part 11 (which mandates electronic record-keeping and documentation accuracy). Companies use DITA's structured validation rules to prevent documentation errors before submission.

Lesson Learned:
Healthcare documentation isn't just about writing—it's about
ensuring regulatory compliance, risk mitigation, and localization
accuracy, making DITA a necessity, not just a preference.

Financial Services & Risk Compliance Docs

How Banks, FinTech, and Financial Compliance Teams Use DITA

In finance, documentation isn't just internal—it's often audited by
regulators, requiring strict adherence to legal and security standards.

I once saw a financial compliance team struggle because their
documentation was spread across multiple systems—Word
documents, PDFs, Excel sheets. Every time a new regulation came into
effect, they had to manually update dozens of documents across
multiple departments. It was a nightmare.

Then they switched to DITA, and everything changed.

»How FinTech Companies Automate Regulatory Docs »» Many FinTech
companies use DITA to manage regulatory updates, ensuring that
financial policies are modular, reusable, and dynamically updated
based on changes in laws.

»Banking Risk Compliance Docs (Basel III, IFRS) »» Large banks use
DITA to track changes in compliance documentation, ensuring that
risk assessment frameworks (Basel III, IFRS, GDPR) are automatically
versioned and traceable.

Lesson Learned:
In finance, manual documentation updates lead to compliance risks—DITA's structured, traceable content ensures that policies remain accurate and auditable.

Manufacturing & Engineering Technical Writing

How the Automotive and Industrial Sectors Use DITA

In engineering-heavy industries, documentation needs to be highly structured, modular, and integrated into digital platforms.

I once saw a manufacturing company manually rewriting sections of user manuals every time a product was updated. The problem? Their documentation was unstructured, making content reuse impossible.

Once they migrated to DITA, everything became modular—if a machine part specification changed, they simply updated one topic, and it propagated across all related documents.

⇥Automotive Industry (ISO 26262 Compliance) ⇥ Companies like Tesla and BMW use DITA to manage structured automotive safety documentation, ensuring that safety protocols remain compliant with international standards (ISO 26262, IATF 16949).

⇢Aerospace and Engineering Firms ⇢ Many engineering firms integrate DITA with CAD software, ensuring that product manuals dynamically update when a machine part design is modified.

Lesson Learned:
DITA eliminates manual updates, making technical documentation automatically reusable and version-controlled in engineering industries.

Seeing how DITA works in real industries changed my perspective—it's not just a structured content model, but a scalable solution for complex documentation challenges.

✓ For software and APIs, DITA enables automation and developer-friendly documentation.
✓ In healthcare, it ensures compliance and accuracy in regulated industries.
✓ For finance, it prevents compliance risks by ensuring up-to-date policies.
✓ In manufacturing, it enables reusable, version-controlled content.

DITA isn't just for technical writers—it's for businesses that rely on documentation as a core part of their operations.

Next, let's explore how DITA fits into Agile and DevOps workflows, where documentation needs to be continuous, automated, and always in sync with development teams.

DITA in Agile and DevOps Documentation

When I first started working with Agile teams, I noticed something: documentation was always behind development.

Developers moved fast—sprints every two weeks, continuous code deployments, and ever-evolving features. But documentation? It was treated like an afterthought. By the time docs were written, the product had already changed.

That's when I realized that traditional documentation workflows just don't work in Agile environments.

DITA, with its modularity, automation, and version control, fits perfectly into Agile and DevOps pipelines, making documentation as continuous as code itself.

This section covers how teams use DITA for Agile and DevOps workflows, ensuring that documentation stays in sync with rapid development cycles.

How Agile Documentation Differs from Traditional Docs?

In traditional development, documentation followed a waterfall approach—first, the product was built, then documentation was written.

In Agile, everything changes.

» Continuous development means continuous documentation.
» Instead of big releases, updates happen in small iterations.
» Content needs to be modular, reusable, and easy to update.

Example: Traditional vs. Agile Documentation Workflow

Aspect	Traditional Docs	Agile Docs

Workflow	Written after the product is built	Written alongside development
Update Cycle	Large, infrequent updates	Small, frequent updates
Structure	Long, linear documents	Modular, reusable content
Publishing	Manual, time-consuming	Automated, integrated with DevOps

This is where DITA's structured, topic-based approach shines.

With DITA, we don't have to rewrite entire manuals—we just update specific topics that are affected by new development changes.

Using DITA for Continuous Documentation in DevOps

One of the best real-world examples of DITA-driven Agile documentation comes from Red Hat.

I once worked with a team using Markdown-based documentation, but they constantly struggled with content updates and consistency across multiple products. Red Hat solved this problem with DITA.

»How Red Hat Uses DITA for CI/CD Docs
 >>DITA topics are stored in a Git repository, versioned alongside

source code.
 >>Content updates are automated using CI/CD pipelines, just like software builds.
 >>Documentation changes undergo automated validation and publishing, ensuring no outdated content gets deployed.

This means documentation keeps up with development, without relying on manual intervention.

Automating Documentation Updates in DevOps Pipelines

Most teams struggle with keeping documentation updated because they rely on manual editing and publishing.

The DITA Solution: Automating Docs with Git-Based Workflows

»Step 1: Store DITA content in a Git repository.
»Step 2: Link documentation updates with code commits.
»Step 3: Automate the build process (CI/CD) to publish docs whenever code changes.

Example: A Git-Based DITA Workflow

1. Developer makes a code change.
2. Documentation team updates the relevant DITA topics.
3. GitHub Actions automatically triggers a validation check.
4. DITA Open Toolkit (DITA-OT) generates the output (PDF, HTML, etc.).
5. Updated docs are deployed to the live site automatically.

This workflow ensures that documentation is always up-to-date, without requiring a manual publishing process.

DITA in CI/CD

DITA fits seamlessly into modern DevOps workflows, allowing teams to automate documentation builds in tools like Jenkins, GitHub Actions, and GitLab CI/CD.

Example: Automating DITA Builds in GitHub Actions

Here's how a GitHub Actions pipeline can automatically process DITA content whenever changes are committed.

```yaml
name: DITA Docs Build

on:
  push:
    branches:
      - main

jobs:
  build:
    runs-on: ubuntu-latest

    steps:
      - name: Checkout repository
        uses: actions/checkout@v2

      - name: Set up DITA-OT
        run: |
          wget
https://github.com/dita-ot/dita-ot/releases/download/3
.7.4/dita-ot-3.7.4.zip
          unzip dita-ot-3.7.4.zip
          export PATH=$PATH:$(pwd)/dita-ot-3.7.4/bin

      - name: Generate Documentation
        run: dita -i docs.ditamap -f html5 -o output/

      - name: Deploy to Documentation Server
        run: rsync -av output/
docs-server:/var/www/docs
```

>>What This Does:

- Triggers a documentation build whenever a change is pushed to `main`.
- Downloads and installs DITA-OT.
- Generates structured documentation (HTML5 format).
- Deploys the updated docs to a live server.

This completely automates the publishing process, ensuring that documentation is always in sync with code changes.

Agile documentation isn't about writing faster—it's about writing smarter.

DITA makes documentation continuous, just like code. Instead of static manuals, we now have dynamic, automated, and always up-to-date documentation pipelines.

✓ Developers can focus on code, knowing documentation updates will follow automatically.
✓ Writers don't have to rewrite entire documents—just update specific DITA topics.
✓ Publishing is no longer a manual process—it's fully automated through CI/CD pipelines.

This is why DITA isn't just a documentation framework—it's a DevOps-friendly system for managing structured content at scale.

Next, let's look at where DITA is headed in the future—AI, automation, and structured content beyond XML.

AI, Automation, and Structured Content

I've been working with structured content for a long time now, and if there's one thing I've learned, it's that technology never stops evolving.

A few years ago, DITA was considered cutting-edge for large-scale technical documentation, but today, we're seeing AI-driven authoring, headless CMS integrations, and the rise of structured content beyond XML.

What's next?

This section isn't about hypothetical predictions—it's about real changes happening right now and how we, as technical writers and content strategists, should adapt.

The Rise of AI-Assisted Technical Writing

For years, writing documentation has been a manual process—subject matter experts (SMEs) explain how a system works, writers translate that knowledge into structured content, and the content goes through rounds of review before publishing.

Now, AI is becoming an active part of the authoring workflow.

How Companies Are Using AI for DITA Documentation?

»Adobe's AI-Powered Authoring Tools » Adobe is integrating AI into RoboHelp and FrameMaker, allowing AI-driven content suggestions and smart tagging for metadata enrichment.

»IBM's Watson for Technical Writing » IBM uses AI to analyze existing DITA content and suggest missing topics, ensuring documentation coverage for all user scenarios.

»Google's AI for API Documentation » Google uses machine learning models to generate API documentation drafts, reducing the workload for writers and ensuring consistency across products.

But AI isn't perfect, and that's where training AI models with custom datasets becomes crucial.

Training AI for DITA-Assisted Authoring

One of the biggest challenges with AI-generated content is that it lacks context. AI doesn't "understand" DITA unless you train it properly.

How Do You Train AI for Technical Writing?

1. Feed AI Models with Pre-Existing DITA Content

>Upload structured DITA XML files into the AI system.

>Let the AI learn from properly written topics, metadata structures, and conditional processing rules.

2. Define Writing Guidelines for AI

> AI must follow the DITA style guide—that means no passive voice, precise terminology, and structured modular content.

> Provide clear examples of Concept, Task, and Reference topics so AI learns how to classify content.

3. Set Up AI for Metadata Generation

> Train AI models to suggest relevant metadata for each topic.

> Example: If a DITA topic is about API authentication, the AI should automatically tag it with `security, API, authentication`.

4. Integrate AI in Authoring Tools

> AI should not replace human writers, but assist them—providing content suggestions, improving consistency, and identifying missing documentation gaps.

> AI-powered tools like ChatGPT, Claude, and Grammarly Business are already being used for content validation and improvement.

AI is only as good as the data it's trained on—the more high-quality DITA content you provide, the more useful AI will be.

DITA and Headless CMS: The Future of Content Delivery

There was a time when documentation meant PDFs and static HTML pages.

Today? Content delivery is dynamic.

With the rise of headless CMS platforms, structured content is no longer just for documentation—it's being used for APIs, chatbots, voice assistants, and multi-channel publishing.

Case Study: Contentful, Sanity.io, and Strapi

»Contentful (API-First Documentation Delivery) » Uses DITA-based structured content to serve documentation dynamically to websites, apps, and embedded systems.

»Sanity.io (Structured Content for AI Chatbots) » Sanity's content models are similar to DITA maps, ensuring that structured responses can be served through chatbots and AI-driven support platforms.

»Strapi (Multi-Channel Content Distribution) » Companies are now feeding structured content into AI-powered search engines, product knowledge bases, and support automation workflows.

What This Means for DITA?

>>Structured content will go beyond traditional documentation.
>>DITA outputs will be served through APIs, not just HTML or PDF.
>>Future-proofing DITA means thinking about AI-driven content consumption.

The Next Evolution of XML & Structured Authoring

Every few years, someone asks:
Is XML going away? Will JSON replace DITA?

The answer? Not anytime soon.

While JSON is becoming the standard for APIs and data exchange, it lacks the built-in structure that makes DITA so powerful for documentation.

Will JSON Ever Replace XML in DITA?

» JSON is great for APIs, but lacks content hierarchy » DITA maps relationships between topics, while JSON is flat and unstructured.
» XML is still the gold standard for structured content reuse » Even headless CMS platforms store structured content in XML, proving its long-term viability.
» Hybrid approaches will emerge » Some companies are exploring hybrid models where JSON is used for lightweight content, and XML remains for structured, reusable documents.

Final Takeaway:
XML isn't dying—it's evolving. DITA will likely continue to be XML-based, but expect more integrations with JSON-driven platforms in the future.

Predictions for the Future of Technical Writing with DITA

So, where is DITA heading in the next decade?

1. **AI-Powered Authoring Will Become the Norm.**

   >AI won't replace writers but will become an integral part of documentation workflows.

   >AI-assisted tagging, metadata generation, and content summarization will be key features in future DITA tools.

2. **DITA Content Will Be Delivered via APIs.**

   Documentation won't be limited to PDFs and web pages—it will be served dynamically through AI chatbots, voice assistants, and API-driven platforms.

3. **Automation Will Drive Continuous Documentation**

   Just like DevOps automates software delivery, DITA will be automated through CI/CD workflows—no more manual publishing, just continuous updates.

4. **Structured Content Will Expand Beyond Documentation**

   Companies will repurpose structured DITA content for AI knowledge bases, customer support automation, and multi-platform content delivery.

5. **The Next Big Shift? AI + Structured Authoring Will Converge**

   AI models will be trained to assist writers with structured authoring, providing content suggestions that follow DITA guidelines automatically.

I've seen DITA evolve over the years, and if one thing is certain, it's this:

1. Structured content isn't going away—it's becoming more essential than ever.
2. AI is changing how we write, but structured authoring will always need human expertise.
3. The future of DITA lies in automation, AI-driven content, and API-powered documentation delivery.

As technical writers, we must embrace these changes, not fear them.

The next decade of technical writing will be driven by AI, automation, and structured content—and DITA will be at the heart of it all.

Chapter 7

APPENDICES

The following appendices provide additional insights, references, and tools to supplement the main content of this book. Whether you are a beginner in DITA or an experienced technical writer looking for best practices, these sections offer valuable resources to help deepen your understanding.

Appendix A: Glossary of Terms

Understanding DITA requires familiarity with key terms. This glossary defines the most frequently used terms in DITA and structured content authoring.

Key Terminology

- DITA (Darwin Information Typing Architecture) – An XML-based architecture for authoring, managing, and delivering structured technical content.
- Topic – The fundamental building block of DITA, representing a single piece of information.
- DITA Map – A structure that organizes multiple topics into a document.
- Specialization – The process of extending DITA to create new topic types or domains tailored for specific industries.

- Metadata – Information that describes content, helping with categorization, searchability, and dynamic publishing.
- Conref (Content Reference) – A method for reusing content dynamically across different topics or maps.
- Keyref (Key Reference) – A mechanism for indirect linking and content reuse in DITA.
- DITA Open Toolkit (DITA-OT) – An open-source tool used for transforming DITA content into different output formats such as HTML, PDF, and ePub.
- Conditional Processing – The ability to filter and customize content dynamically for different audiences or formats.
- XML (Extensible Markup Language) – A markup language used for structuring and managing content in a machine-readable format.
- DITAVAL – A file format that defines conditions for filtering content in DITA publishing.
- CCMS (Component Content Management System) – A content management system optimized for structured content and modular authoring.

Appendix B: DITA Specification & Versioning

B.1 About the Specification Source

DITA is maintained as an OASIS open standard, evolving through multiple iterations.

B.2 Changes from Previous Versions

This section provides an overview of key changes across DITA versions:

B.2.1 Changes from DITA 1.2 to DITA 1.3

- Introduction of branch filtering for advanced content reuse.
- Improved scalability with new metadata attributes.

- Enhanced support for lightweight DITA to simplify adoption.

B.2.2 Changes from DITA 1.1 to DITA 1.2

- Expansion of specialization capabilities.
- Introduction of key-based referencing (keyref).
- Refinements to conditional processing for multi-channel publishing.

B.2.3 Changes from DITA 1.0 to DITA 1.1

- Standardization of metadata attributes.
- Improved support for localization workflows.
- Addition of DITA constraints for content standardization.

B.3 File Naming Conventions

DITA follows standardized naming conventions to ensure consistency in file organization and reference management.

- Topic files: Use lowercase names with underscores (e.g., `user_guide.dita`).
- DITA maps: Use the `.ditamap` extension (e.g., `product_manual.ditamap`).
- Image files: Stored in a `/media` or `/images` directory.

B.4 Migrating to New Versions of DITA

Migration strategies vary depending on the version upgrade.

B.4.1 Migrating from DITA 1.2 to 1.3

- Update metadata structures to leverage new attributes.
- Review specialization constraints for compatibility.

B.4.2 Migrating from DITA 1.1 to 1.2

- Ensure support for key-based referencing.
- Convert manual cross-references into keyrefs for better maintainability.

B.5 Considerations for Generalizing <foreign> Elements

DITA allows <foreign> elements for embedding non-DITA XML, but these should be managed carefully to maintain document integrity.

B.6 Element-by-Element Recommendations for Translators

Translation best practices ensure that content remains accurate and structured across different languages.

Appendix C: DITA Tools and Resources

This section provides an extensive list of authoring tools, resources, and software that can enhance your work with DITA.

C.1 Authoring Tools

Authoring tools play a crucial role in creating, managing, and publishing DITA-based content. These tools help technical writers, content architects, and documentation teams streamline structured content workflows. Below is a detailed breakdown of widely used DITA authoring tools, their unique features, and how they fit into different documentation workflows.

Oxygen XML Editor

Oxygen XML Editor is one of the most powerful and widely used DITA authoring tools. It provides a comprehensive suite of features designed specifically for structured content creation, validation, and publishing.

Key Features:

✓ Full DITA Support – Oxygen XML Editor comes with built-in DITA support, including templates for different topic types (Concept, Task, Reference), maps, and key references.
✓ Real-time Validation – Ensures that XML documents conform to the DITA standard, with automatic error detection.
✓ WYSIWYG Author Mode – Offers a user-friendly interface for writers who prefer a visual editor over raw XML editing.
✓ Content Reuse Management – Supports conrefs, keyrefs, and conditional processing to enhance content modularity.
✓ Integrated DITA Open Toolkit (DITA-OT) – Allows direct transformation of DITA content into multiple output formats, including PDF, HTML, and ePub.
✓ Collaboration Features – Oxygen XML Web Author enables real-time collaborative editing with version control integration (Git, SVN).

Best Use Case:

Oxygen XML Editor is best suited for large-scale technical documentation teams that require highly structured content workflows, robust validation, and flexibility in publishing outputs.

XMetaL Author

XMetaL Author is a structured XML editor designed specifically for technical documentation teams that work with DITA and other structured content models. It provides a balance between ease of use and advanced XML control.

Key Features:

✓ Intuitive XML Editing – Provides both a raw XML editor and a user-friendly WYSIWYG interface for content creation.
✓ Seamless DITA Authoring – Comes with built-in DITA templates and structured topic support.

✓ Conditional Content Management – Allows technical writers to define audience-specific filtering rules.
✓ Integration with CMS and Publishing Systems – Connects with Component Content Management Systems (CCMS) and publishing pipelines.
✓ Custom Scripting & Macros – Supports automation and customization for repetitive documentation tasks.

Best Use Case:

XMetaL Author is ideal for organizations transitioning from unstructured to structured authoring, especially those that need a balance between a user-friendly interface and raw XML control.

Arbortext Editor

Arbortext Editor is an enterprise-grade XML and DITA authoring tool designed for regulated industries such as healthcare, finance, aerospace, and manufacturing.

Key Features:

✓ Advanced Structured Authoring – Provides full support for DITA, S1000D, and other structured content models.
✓ Regulatory Compliance Support – Helps organizations maintain strict content validation and compliance requirements.
✓ Seamless CMS Integration – Works with Windchill, Documentum, and other enterprise content management systems.
✓ Dynamic Content Reuse – Enables content sharing and multi-channel publishing across large enterprises.
✓ Single-Sourcing for Multilingual Publishing – Supports localized content management with automated translation workflows.

Best Use Case:

Arbortext Editor is best suited for highly regulated industries that require strict document control, compliance validation, and scalable content reuse.

DITA Open Toolkit (DITA-OT)

DITA Open Toolkit (DITA-OT) is an open-source publishing engine that transforms DITA XML into various output formats. Unlike other tools in this list, DITA-OT is not an authoring tool but a publishing framework.

Key Features:

✓ Multi-Format Output Generation – Converts DITA content into PDF, HTML5, ePub, Microsoft Help (CHM), and Markdown.
✓ Highly Customizable – Supports custom XSLT and CSS for transforming structured content into branded output.
✓ Plug-in Support – Enables organizations to extend functionality with third-party DITA-OT plug-ins.
✓ Command-Line and Automated Publishing – Ideal for batch processing, CI/CD workflows, and automated documentation pipelines.

Best Use Case:

DITA-OT is essential for technical writers and documentation engineers who need a flexible, customizable publishing tool for automating content delivery.

Adobe FrameMaker

Adobe FrameMaker is a professional desktop publishing tool that includes native DITA support, making it a good choice for organizations looking for a hybrid structured/unstructured content workflow.

Key Features:

✓ Structured and Unstructured Authoring – Supports both DITA XML and traditional word-processing workflows.

✓ Robust Print & PDF Publishing – Ideal for creating high-quality print documentation and manuals.

✓ Responsive HTML5 Output – Converts structured content into mobile-friendly, web-based documentation.

✓ Integration with Adobe CC & CMS – Connects with Adobe Experience Manager and third-party CCMS platforms.

✓ Content Review & Collaboration – Allows multiple users to review and annotate content before final publishing.

Best Use Case:

Adobe FrameMaker is best for organizations that need both traditional document authoring and structured DITA workflows with strong PDF and print output capabilities.

Choosing the Right DITA Authoring Tool

Each authoring tool has its strengths and is suited to different types of documentation teams:

- For Enterprise Teams: » Oxygen XML Editor or Arbortext Editor
- For Teams New to DITA: » XMetaL Author or Adobe FrameMaker
- For Automated Publishing Pipelines: » DITA-OT
- For Compliance & Regulatory Docs: » Arbortext Editor

Selecting the right tool depends on workflow complexity, content reuse needs, automation requirements, and publishing goals. If customization and automation are essential, DITA-OT may be the best choice, while Oxygen XML Editor is best for organizations with highly structured content workflows.

C.2 Learning Resources

- OASIS DITA Standard Documentation – The official reference for DITA implementation.
- DITA XML Learning Center – An online hub for tutorials and case studies.
- LinkedIn DITA User Group – A professional network for discussing DITA best practices.
- DITA Bootcamp Course – A structured online learning course for mastering DITA.

Appendix D: Sample DITA Code

This section includes real-world examples of DITA topic structures, maps, and specialization implementations.

D.1 Sample DITA Topic

A basic example of a DITA topic:

```xml
<topic id="introduction">
  <title>Understanding DITA</title>
  <shortdesc>DITA is a structured content framework
for technical documentation.</shortdesc>
  <body>
    <section>
      <title>What is DITA?</title>
      <p>DITA enables modular, reusable, and scalable
documentation.</p>
    </section>
  </body>
</topic>
```

D.2 Sample DITA Map

A hierarchical structure linking multiple topics:

```
<map>
  <title>Product Documentation</title>
  <topicref href="introduction.dita"/>
  <topicref href="installation_guide.dita"/>
  <topicref href="user_manual.dita"/>
</map>
```

D.3 Sample DITA Specialization

A specialized DITA task type:

```
<!DOCTYPE mytask PUBLIC "-//OASIS//DTD DITA Task//EN"
"task.dtd">
<mytask id="custom_task">
  <title>Perform Custom Action</title>
  <body>
    <steps>
      <step>
        <cmd>Open settings panel</cmd>
      </step>
      <step>
        <cmd>Enable advanced options</cmd>
      </step>
    </steps>
  </body>
</mytask>
```

Appendix E: DITA Best Practices Checklist

E.1 Writing Best Practices

- Maintain consistent terminology across documents.
- Use short, clear, and structured sentences.
- Follow topic-based authoring principles.

E.2 Content Reuse Strategies

- Implement conrefs and keyrefs to avoid redundancy.
- Leverage DITAVAL files for dynamic filtering.

E.3 Publishing & Formatting

- Customize DITA-OT transformations for branding and styling.
- Ensure accessibility compliance with structured content guidelines.

This book has covered everything from foundational DITA concepts to advanced implementation strategies. But as with any technology, DITA is always evolving.

My advice? Keep learning, stay curious, and continue refining your structured content workflows. The best technical writers and content architects are those who embrace new tools, experiment with automation, and always seek to improve.

Good luck on your DITA journey!

One Final Note

Writing this book has been more than just compiling facts about DITA—it has been about translating years of hands-on experience into something structured, something that can genuinely help someone like you, who is either just beginning their journey or looking to refine their expertise in structured content.

If you've made it this far, I want you to pause for a moment and acknowledge your progress. Understanding DITA, let alone mastering it, isn't a casual endeavor. It's a shift in the way we think about documentation—how we structure it, how we write, and how we deliver content at scale. By reading this book, you've already moved ahead of many who still rely on fragmented, inefficient documentation workflows.

What Comes Next?

Learning DITA isn't a one-time event. You will keep discovering new things, new challenges, and new ways to optimize your content strategy. The key is experimentation—don't just stop at what's in this book. Push the boundaries. Try specialization if you haven't already. Experiment with automated workflows. See how AI can assist in content validation. The more you apply, the more intuitive it all becomes.

The best technical writers, information architects, and documentation engineers aren't those who simply follow best practices—they are the ones who question them, who seek better ways to organize, manage, and publish content.

A Message for the Future DITA Experts

If there's one thing I want you to take away from this book, it's this: DITA is not just about XML. It's about the future of structured communication.

As industries move toward automation, AI-driven content processing, and headless CMS platforms, structured content will become even more critical. Those who master DITA today will be the ones leading documentation and content management strategies in the coming years.

I truly hope this book has given you a strong foundation—not just in understanding DITA but in developing the right mindset to tackle any structured content challenge. And remember, the learning never stops.

Whether you use DITA for API documentation, enterprise manuals, regulatory compliance, or product content, your work is what enables others to understand, learn, and build.

So, keep experimenting. Keep learning. And most importantly—keep writing.

-   Snehasish Konger

Note